Translation: A Guide to t Practice of Crafting Targ

CW01501909

This practical guide by two experienced translators and translation tutors explores aspects of time, context and culture in a range of translated literary texts, including novels, memoirs, poems and plays. Reflective analytical sections are complemented by a variety of practical tasks that reflect the book's craft-based approach. Providing a dual focus on both analysis and creativity, this volume helps readers to develop two different skill sets required for translation: **deconstruction** and **reconstruction**.

To learn how to analyse or deconstruct a **source text (ST)**, the tasks include translating and editing, comparison and analysis of **source language (SL)** texts and translations and critiquing or improving **target language (TL)** texts produced by translators from different times. A range of **creative writing** challenges reveal the secrets writers use to hook their readers. Whatever language readers translate into, these insights will help them to find their own writer's voice, making them better equipped to recreate another author's voice, whatever the time or cultural context.

This is the essential guide to improving target texts for all translators and students of translation.

Stella Cragie is a Qualified Member of the Institute of Translation and Interpreting and is an ISO 17100:215-qualified translator. She was for many years a principal lecturer in translation at the University of Westminster, where she remains a visiting lecturer. She is also a freelance translator, working from French, Italian and Romanian into English. She was the lead author of the second edition of *Thinking Italian Translation*, published in 2016, and of *Thinking English Translation*, published in 2018, and has a special interest in art history and antiques.

Ann Pattison is a Fellow of the Institute of Translation and Interpreting and is an ISO 17100:215-qualified translator. She has taught translation at the University of Surrey, London Metropolitan University and Imperial College and is a former senior lecturer in translation at the University of Westminster. She now works as a freelance translator, editor and writer. She was co-author of *Thinking English Translation*, published in 2018. Her novel *Notes Out of Time* was published on lulu.com, and she has compiled two anthologies of work by members of Sutton Writers. Ann has also had two plays performed in Sutton.

Translation: A Guide to the Practice of Crafting Target Texts

STELLA CRAGIE AND ANN PATTISON

Routledge
Taylor & Francis Group

LONDON AND NEW YORK

First published 2020
by Routledge
2 Park Square, Milton Park, Abingdon, Oxon OX14 4RN

and by Routledge
52 Vanderbilt Avenue, New York, NY 10017

Routledge is an imprint of the Taylor & Francis Group, an informa business.

British Library Cataloguing-in-Publication Data
A catalogue record for this book is available from the British Library

Library of Congress Cataloging-in-Publication Data
Names: Cragie, Stella, author. | Pattison, Ann, author.
Title: Translation, a guide to the practice of crafting target texts / Stella
    Cragie and Ann Pattison.
Description: 1. | New York : Taylor and Francis, 2020. | Includes
    bibliographical references and index.
Identifiers: LCCN 2019034246 | ISBN 9781138354203 (hardback) |
    ISBN 9781138354357 (paperback) | ISBN 9780367855451 (ebook)
Subjects: LCSH: Translating and interpreting—Study and teaching. |
    Translating and interpreting—Methodology. | Language arts (Higher)—
    Correlation with content subjects.
Classification: LCC P306.5 .C724 2020 | DDC 418/.04—dc23
LC record available at https://lccn.loc.gov/2019034246

ISBN: 978-1-138-35420-3 (hbk)
ISBN: 978-1-138-35435-7 (pbk)
ISBN: 978-0-367-85545-1 (ebk)

Typeset in Akzidenz Grotesk
by Apex CoVantage, LLC

Contents

Acknowledgements

The authors and publisher would like to thank the following translators for their invaluable contributions to the annotated translations in Chapter 3: Philippe Galinier (MA, MCIL, MITI), Dr Elsa Huertas-Barros (Lecturer in Translation Studies, University of Westminster), Susanne James (MA, MCIL, FHEA), Susan M. Neve (BA, CIOL Dip. Trans) and Marina Donarini-Edwards (MA). Thanks must also go to the writer Claudia Forero and the philosophical researchers Dr Arkady Izvekov, International University, Moscow, and Professor Nadezda Golik, St Petersburg State University, for providing us with copies of their work for inclusion in Chapter 3 and the Appendix.

We are likewise indebted to Philippe Portier (Professor at the Ecole pratique des hautes études-PSL), to Pierre-Jean Luizard (Research Director at GSRL, a section within CNRS in Paris) and to Valentine Zuber (Professor at the Ecole pratique des hautes études-PSL) for permission to use extracts from their presentations in the field of social sciences. Claudia Strachan, MA, was also a useful source for the comparison of letter-writing conventions in English and German at the time of World War I.

We very much appreciate the kind support Ian Higgins gave us and were delighted to be able to include two of his translations of French poetry, together with his very enlightening commentaries. Considerable advice, encouragement and information was also provided by members of Sutton Writers, in particular Claudia Forero and Barbara Saunders, who kindly helped with queries for Chapters 3 and 4. Many thanks are also due to all of those who took the time to answer our questions.

Introduction

SCOPE AND OBJECTIVES

We consider translation to be a craft that requires two very different skill sets. The first requires the ability to analyse the source text – to *deconstruct* it, in fact – whereas the second involves using creativity to recreate the author's world in the **target text**, that is, to *reconstruct* it. This practical guide aims to help readers to develop both critical awareness and creative writing skills. These two strands therefore run in parallel through the book.

Deconstruction involves reading and analysis of the source text aimed at critical awareness, through creation of a model for identifying characteristics of the source text that will be relevant or crucial in the transfer of information, style and cultural aspects from the source language into the target language. **Reconstruction** involves active engagement and dialogue with the source text, leading to transfer into and production of the target text. *Deconstruction* is a reflective process, while *reconstruction* is a creative one (but also a reflective one). Our use of the term *deconstruction* differs from the one proposed by the philosopher Jacques Derrida: he considered it a "form of philosophical and literary analysis ... that questions the fundamental conceptual distinctions, or 'oppositions', in western philosophical and literary texts" (*Encyclopaedia Britannia* online; for further information on this concept see www.britannica.com/topic/deconstruction).

Our guide will be of particular interest to postgraduate and final-year undergraduate students of translation, world literature and creative writing at universities in the UK and abroad. It can be used to support translation or literature seminars in a higher education context or for independent study. It will also be useful for the continuing professional development of professional translators who want to add literary and semi-literary texts to their specialist subjects.

The main analytical focus is on how the various perspectives of **time**, **context** and **culture** create the framework for a literary or semi-literary type of text and influence the choices made by the translator. We consider the significance of these perspectives, helping readers to devise appropriate strategies for tackling the challenges they present, which are reflected in the texts and genres selected for analysis. These include literary fiction, crime fiction, memoirs, drama and academic articles on art, culture and social history.

To make it easier for you to identify key features in the source text, we have designed a practical model in the form of a table which lists the criteria translators need to consider in their analysis. This table is similar to those we devised for *Thinking English Translation* (Routledge, 2018), but we have adapted it to focus in particular on time, context and culture – perspectives which are highly relevant to literary and semi-literary texts.

To help you to write annotations or commentaries as part of an undergraduate or postgraduate degree, we expand the features highlighted in the analytical model to include simple and relevant explanations of concepts from linguistics, **literary criticism** and **literary theory**.

The practical tasks include analysing source texts, translating, editing and **critique** of existing translations, in addition to a range of open-ended complementary tasks, such as eliciting opinions, reflections, revisions and other translation-related exercises through the "Pause for thought" boxes situated at strategic points in the discussions in the chapters.

The main source and target languages covered include English, French, German, Italian and Spanish.

In the creative strand of the book, we adopt a craft-based approach, with a variety of practical tasks designed to develop the translator's role as a creative or at least semi-creative writer. These tasks include exercises to help you improve your word-power, such as exploring synonyms and semantic fields, and writing challenges that will enable you to develop your own writing voice, which you need to find before you can truly identify and replicate another writer's voice and, ideally, acquire the mindset of a writer.

These exercises are also devised to instil stylistic awareness. Many of them specifically echo the analytical focus of the book on the three **themes** of time, context and culture, yet present them from a writer's perspective. A typical exercise involves describing a childhood memory in the past tense and then rewriting it in the present tense. Another task asks you to transpose what you have written into a different cultural and/or historical setting.

The expected **learning outcomes** are as follows:

1 Developing an awareness of the role of time, context and cultural perspectives in literary and semi-literary texts and in translation;
2 Acquiring skills in analysing both source and target texts, with an emphasis on the timeframe/s and cultural setting/s, and exploring how these aspects can influence translation choices, in particular lexis, register and style;
3 Understanding how language use changes over time and impacts on translation approaches, in particular on the target language;
4 Gaining an understanding of the creative writing process and of literary theory;

5 Becoming familiar with the frameworks for analysis and comparison, using these to critique the reader's own translations and those by other practitioners;

6 Applying analytical skills to the translation process;

7 Developing and implementing appropriate strategies for tackling translation challenges;

8 Learning how to make lexical choices appropriate to the time of writing and/or translation;

9 Acquiring skills in identifying and replicating another writer's voice;

10 Achieving a more natural writing style in the target language, avoiding any hint of "**translationese**."

The book is structured as follows:

- **Introduction**
- **Chapter 1: Groundworks**
- **Chapter 2: Exploring time, context and culture through language**
- **Chapter 3: Analysing, translating, comparing, editing**

  Part 1: Analyses of English texts
  Part 2: Annotated translations
  Part 3: Translation comparisons
  Part 4: Editing translations: a few tips

- **Chapter 4: How to enhance your writing skills**
- **Conclusion**
- **Appendix**
- **Glossary**
- **Bibliography**
- **Index**

CHAPTER 1

Groundworks

The book's orientation is both writer-centred and translator-centred, since our objective is to examine literary and semi-literary texts and translations with a translator's critical eye and a writer's well-toned creative muscle (the word *muscle* is a deliberate choice because writers have to hone their skills with a regular workout in the same way as runners have to perform a whole sequence of warm-up exercises before they take part in a race).

Both writer and translator need to be aware of how the language they are using relates to the time and cultural context in which the text is set. Therefore, particular attention is given to language change, variations in language that are dependent on social context, the various aspects of **meaning** and inter-cultural communication.

Many writers over the centuries were able to improve their craft by studying translations of the classics and even attempting to produce a new translation of their own. In the history of European literature, there are a number of examples of such writer-translators, ranging from the Roman orator Quintilian to the modern-day poet Seamus Heaney or the author Michael Frayn, via Mallarmé, Voltaire and even Montesquieu, who feared that translation could have a negative effect on a writer's creativity (Ann Pattison *Painting with Words*, in *Translation and Creativity: Perspectives on Creative Writing and Translation Studies*, edited by Eugenia Loffredo and Manuela Perteghella, 2006, Continuum: London).

The legacy of world literature in translation and the controversy surrounding old and new translations of seminal works, such as Simone de Beauvoir's *The Second Sex*, have provided us with a wealth of material to demonstrate how both *the time of writing* and *the cultural environment prevalent at the time of translation*, in addition to the timeframes used in the work, can affect not only the translation **strategy** and approach but also the way a particular work is received.

To facilitate the process of deconstruction, we use analysis and comparison based on interactions between the perspectives of time, context and culture: imagine a triangle with time at the top and context and culture at the bottom. The triangle symbolises the interaction of these perspectives. In broad terms, *Time* explores *WHEN*; *Context* looks at *WHAT*, *WHERE* and *WHO*; *Culture* involves the values and viewpoints of the stakeholders (i.e., the author/narrator, characters/ actors and translator/s).

Understanding these perspectives is central to analysis of a literary or semi-literary work (a poem, a play, a novel, a memoir or a piece of scholarly writing).

DEFINITIONS

Time takes pride of place in the trio of perspectives because it acts as a benchmark or regulator of the plot/theme of the work, by creating a sequence of timeframes to enable the plot/theme to develop. The diversity of timeframes in fiction, for instance, generates a complex web of interaction and flow, which may be linear, circular, forward, backward or any combination of these dynamics. In modern and contemporary literature, the importance of time factors has grown significantly, hand in hand with the development of visual media (films or televised works in particular). In novels written in the nineteenth and early twentieth century, the author's creative effort and skills generally tended to develop the action through a chronological sequence of scenes; readers progressed through these scenes, imagining the events, and the only concrete visual stimuli were probably book illustrations. The theatre and opera, however, were already combining words (and music) into more "realistic" and direct forms of visual representation, with actors and singers performing on stage, in costume and with scenery, thus providing the audience with visual stimuli. Some modern and contemporary fiction (for example, thrillers) appears particularly "visually driven" in its filmic manipulation and sequencing of timeframes. For example, the thrillers written by Eric Ambler in the late 1930s may be "semi-consciously written as film scripts. . . . Ambler was directly involved in the cinema, and crafted his books directly in terms of their filmability" (a comment by Norman Stone from the Introduction to Ambler's *Journey into Fear*, published in 1940 and made into a film produced by Orson Welles in 1942).

But time is not limited to the timeframes expressed in the work itself; there are time factors that are external to the work, such as the moment in time when it was written, published and translated (where applicable), as well as less definable time factors (such as reading).

The stories recounted in the Icelandic sagas, for instance, mostly took place in Iceland in the ninth, tenth and early eleventh centuries and were based on historical events. They were part of an oral tradition that helped to forge Iceland's national identity, but it was not until the thirteenth or fourteenth centuries that they were recorded in written form. It was even later, in the eighteenth century, that translations from Old Norse into European languages began to appear. (Source: Oscar Wergeland *Guide to the classics: the Icelandic saga* 14.08.2016 http://theconversation.com/guide-to-the-classics-the-icelandic-saga-63112).

The anonymous mediaeval German love poem that appears below is believed to have been written in the late twelfth century, but the vow of undying love that it expresses is of course timeless. Even so, recreating these sentiments remains a challenge for the translator nine centuries later!

> *Dû bist mîn, ich bin dîn.*
> *des solt dû gewis sîn.*
> *dû bist beslozzen*
> *in mînem herzen,*
> *verlorn ist das sluzzelîn:*
> *dû muost ouch immêr darinne sîn.*

For those who are not familiar with mediaeval German, a literal and semantic rendering of the original poem would be:

> *You are mine, I am thine,*
> *You can be sure of that.*
> *You are locked away*
> *In my heart,*
> *The tiny key is lost,*
> *So there you must always stay.*

One of the present authors was asked to produce a modern English version to be read out at a wedding. The simple yet heartfelt language in which the poem was written helped the translator to visualise the context and gain an idea of what the author might have been like. The voice appeared to be that of someone young and unspoilt, which might justify the use of simple English structures in the translation. But what about the language? Should the **archaic** form "thine" be used for the sake of authenticity and to preserve the rhyme, or would it be better to recreate the rhyme in a different way? If "thine" was thought to be too old-fashioned, could the mediaeval context be echoed by using less modern words in other parts of the poem?

One possible, slightly freer, version was the following:

> *You belong to me, I belong to you,*
> *You need to know that this is true.*

Would this work in a twenty-first century context? The issue with this was that a modern bride might well object to the idea of being described as belonging to anyone!

Another version with a slightly facetious opening that preserved the sounds in the German rhyme was

> *I'm yours, you're mine,*
> *You know that's the bottom line.*
> *You are locked away*

In my heart,
The little key has gone astray,
So there you must always stay.

The translator was keen to preserve the rather quaint and touching tone of the original with "locked away" and "gone astray" but felt there needed to be a modern touch somewhere in the poem, and, if possible, it should scan. She tried to convey the poet's assurances with a more colloquial expression "you know that's the bottom line," but the problem was that it just did not sound romantic. She tried to rectify this by removing "always" from the last line and adding another line to round off the poem. The final, still imperfect, version was

I'm yours, you're mine,
You know that's the bottom line.
In my heart you're locked away
Because the key has gone astray,
And so you'll have to stay.
There till the end of time.

You might like to try to improve on this yourselves, particularly on the second and the last lines.

Pause for thought: Think of a classic novel in your source language that you have seen in a dramatised version. Imagine that you have been asked to produce a new translation of the novel. Do you think the way you "view" the work as a translator might be influenced by the dramatised version, and if so, how?

Just to get you started, consider how you were affected by a recent popular television series; in the UK, for example, Debbie Horsfield's reworking of Winston Graham's *Poldark*, David Farr's version of John Le Carré's *The Night Manager* or Gwyneth Hughes' adaptation of Thackeray's *Vanity Fair* (or literary adaptations for television or the cinema in other languages).

Context can be considered *logistically* as the space where an action, scene or idea takes shape in a specific setting or *linguistically*, where the term refers to the location of a lexical item in its surrounding **discourse**. Even a scholarly article needs some **contextualisation** (such as an introduction, some background or a premise which provides a platform for the definition and development of the theme through arguments, reasoning and information). Context is also an intellectual space, and a psychological one, as we shall see.

In his article on Icelandic sagas (*see page 5*), Oscar Wergeland relates the creation of a new literary form to the context of "the empire writing back to the motherland, in this case Iceland 'writing back' to Norway and to common Scandinavian oral traditions of poetry and story."

> **Pause for thought**: Can you think of a literary work that lacks a specific context (maybe a poem or existentialist piece of literature)? For instance, the mediaeval poem discussed earlier does not have a specific setting, although the language indicates that the poet came from one of the areas where Middle High German was spoken, that is, somewhere in what is now central and southern Germany, Austria or Switzerland. Do you think the lack of context makes the translation process easier or more difficult, or does that simply depend on the work itself?

Culture reflects a historical, geographical, linguistic and social setting; **extra-contextual** circumstances and information; traditions; values; and behaviour. These aspects provide the "local colour" that characterises a specific setting or action, by filling out the picture that the reader forms in his or her own mind (a process we call **visualisation**). It is important to remember that culture is not only relevant to the work itself but also to the author, the critic, the reader and the translator, who all contribute their "**cultural share**" to the environment in which the work exists.

The French intellectual and advocate of structuralism, Roland Barthes, was a major contributor to ideas about culture. In *Le Degré Zéro* (published in 1953), he asserted that "The political significance of writing is not simply a matter of political content or of an author's overt political commitment but also of the work's engagement with a culture's literary ordering of the world" (Jonathan Culler, *Barthes – A Very Short Introduction*, OUP, 2002: 21). He attempted to change the way people think about culture, in particular, history, fashion and literature. The aim of the structuralists was to "shift the focus of critical thinking from subjects to discourse, from authors as sources of meaning to systems of convention operating within the discursive systems of social practice" (2002: 74). This shift in focus undermined the view that the author was "God" and the reader simply someone who processed literature without participating in it. In *Image, Music, Text* (1977), he famously referred to the "death of the author" and suggested that a text was a "multi-dimensional space in which a variety of writings, none of them original, blend and clash" (2002: 2), concluding that we should study texts rather than authors. This sparked a debate about the active role of the reader in which he or she contributes to the text (i.e., has a cultural share, rather than a passive involvement). In this perspective, the reader becomes important as the "repository of conventions, the agent of their application" (2002: 68).

As Hans Berten points out in *Literary Theory – The Basics* (3rd ed. Routledge: 2014), "Finally, after decades of neglect, there is a renewed interest in how readers actually process texts and attribute meaning to them." It is sometimes easy to forget how wide and complex the network of stakeholders of a work can be. This network becomes even more extensive when translations of a work are involved. Therefore, we will also examine the part that stakeholders play in this complex web.

> **Pause for thought**: What "cultural share" does a reader or a translator bring to the work? Imagine translating a favourite novel of yours, and say how your life experience, values, politics, likes and dislikes and so on might affect your attitude and approach to the translation.

The multiple ways in which our three perspectives interact and interweave create what we could call "infrastructure." In Chapter 2, we will look more closely at criteria such as genre, form, discourse, meaning and style to show how language delivers and builds this infrastructure. For example, we consider how different languages use verbs (tenses, other verb forms or sequence of tense) to describe present, past and future actions and states, in direct and indirect speech and explore how tense use can differ significantly between languages. If we take a classic English thriller by Agatha Christie, for example, where the action is narrated in the third person, the tenses are usually in the past (except, of course, in dialogue), whereas in Italian and French, the simple present (or "**historic present**") is often used as the narrative tense of choice, to avoid complex past conditional and subjunctive forms in indirect speech (future in the past) throughout the translation. It is interesting to note, however, that the use of the present historic in narrative is now popular in contemporary fiction in English, probably due to the effect of immediacy it creates (as opposed to the "remoteness" of past tenses). The influence of visual media, such as films, may well be a factor here, resulting in greater convergence between written and oral discourse.

On this issue, Susan Bassnett cites Hilary Mantel's *Wolf Hall* as an example of a novel "written entirely in the present tense." She goes on to remark, "Since then, the historic present has been everywhere" and points out that "Choosing the appropriate tense to use when translating a novel or a short story is not straightforward. A translator has to think about the expectations of the readers, and what they are used to, as well as about what works and does not work in the target language" ("Beyond Words," in *ITI Bulletin*, September–October 2018: 26–27).

RELEVANCE OF TIME

Down the centuries, writers, philosophers and scientists have argued over the concept of time, without resolving "puzzles – such as whether the past and future are real, whether time travel is possible, and the explanation of the direction of time" (Callender, 2001, *Introducing Time – A Graphic Guide*, p. 3). One practical way of defining time is "a continuous passage of existence in which events pass from a state of potentiality in the future, through the present, to a state of finality in the past" (*Collins Reverso Dictionary*, online).

Aristotle considered time simply as a way of measuring motion, where one physical process is related to another (a theory called "relationism"), while Newton distinguished time from its "sensible measure" (i.e., clocks) and considered "real time" as independent of any clock or object in the universe. Another philosopher who contributed to the debate was the physicist Henri Poincaré, who believed there is no such thing as "true time" and that no single way of measuring time is any more reliable than another. In the late nineteenth century, Henri Bergson suggested that the human experience of time was not scientific, describing it as a *flow* (*durée*) involving past, present and future and an experience of existing within that flow. But he also remarked that experiences are not linear and can be *stretched* (an experience can seem longer or shorter than its actual duration); thus, the way time is experienced is unique to each individual. This theory is particularly relevant to narrative or fictive time, where experiences can be manipulated to be longer or shorter to suit the author's plot development. Edmund Husserl took Bergson's ideas further, by focusing on the concept of consciousness, considering consciousness of time as a concatenation of future, past and present. In the twentieth century, "tenseless" and "tensed" theories of time were proposed: the former sees time as a static block, like space, while the latter suggests that time flows, like a dynamic entity. Another way of thinking about time is to consider it as a series of frames of reference, where the speed or flow depends on how frames of reference move in relation to one another. This latter concept is particularly relevant to plot development in fiction in modern and contemporary literature, as authors are usually more innovative in their time sequencing than in earlier traditional literature and classics.

Objectively, we measure time by means of clocks or scientific apparatus, and subjectively, we measure it through our personal experiences and perceptions. "Personal time" is an ordering parameter that defines a person's physical and mental processes. This concept is important for the reader's (and translator's) cultural share, as individual experiences undoubtedly influence the reading or translating of a work. However, while the reader's imagination could be said to experience no real boundaries beyond the storyline (and in poetry, virtually no boundaries at all), translators need to align their imagination and visualisation processes with the source text constraints of language and logic. The "narrower" the frame of reference of the work, the greater the limitations in choice. The translator's skill lies in **decoding** the source text and then combining it with targeted visualisation and imagination to arrive at the most appropriate target language renderings from those available (through practical experience, knowledge and research).

In *The Naïve and Sentimental Novelist* (Faber & Faber, London: 2016), the Nobel Prize-winner Orhan Pamuk sets out his theory of the novel, from both the writer's and the reader's perspective. He explains,

> in novels, time is not the linear and objective time indicated by Aristotle, but the subjective time of the protagonists. Yet in order to determine the relationships among the protagonists, we readers still try to discern – especially when reading densely populated novels – the objective time shared by everyone in the novel.
>
> (2016: 81)

Pause for thought: Find a passage from a favourite novel of yours in a language that you translate from. Read the passage carefully and try to describe the images or arguments the text creates in your mind. Then read the passage again, as a translator. What differences do you notice in the way you "process" each reading?

There are also biological clocks (circadian rhythms) and lunar cycles. But this book is concerned primarily with ways in which time is expressed in literature, so we will focus on temporal relationships with context and culture, with the plot, with readers' expectations and reception and on the translation challenges posed by time, context and culture through language.

A literary work, particularly of fiction, normally creates a microcosm or reality in which the reader "suspends disbelief" in order to enter and participate in the author's world. The representation of time may follow a standard chronological (or linear) development in an attempt to imitate "real life," or it may juxtapose events in the past, present and future with flashes backwards and forwards; the setting may be all in the past, working towards the present and future; it may be set in a past time that is remote compared to the time of writing, based on real events and characters or fictitious ones, or it may be set entirely in the future, as in science fiction. It may even start at the end of the story and work back towards the beginning. David Mitchell's *Cloud Atlas* is an example of a novel structured around multiple timeframes with characters and storylines that stretch from the past to the present and the future and back.

Pause for thought: Can you give examples of any books or plays that use these different timeframes? Are there any other ways of representing time (or the absence of time) in literature that you can think of that are not mentioned here?

To produce an effective translation of a novel, poem or play, we need to enter that "other world" and experience it as realistically as possible through the author's eyes, following the sequencing of actions, events and arguments. Remaining on the outside or on the fringe of the fictive time, action and plot/theme will not help us, as readers and as translators, to evoke, as far as possible, "what the author experienced" when creating the work.

So far, we have looked at time generally, but in narrative works, it is a more intricate and complex phenomenon. In Volume 2 of *Temps et Récit* (Seuil, 1984) by Paul Ricoeur, which appeared in translation as *Time and Narrative* in 1985, published by the University of Chicago Press, time is described as a "a parallel capacity of being divided into the time of the act of narrating and the time of the things narrated" (1985: 5). He also refers to "the fictive experience of time" to express the temporal aspects of what he calls the world of the text and the "ways of inhabiting the world that the texts projects outside of itself" (*ibid:* 6). The idea of multiple timeframes is developed further in a very interesting article (written by Will Greenway in 1983 and published online by Moira Allen in 2017), which highlights the role of time in writing and, in particular, in storytelling. He identifies as many as eight "shades of time" in narrative, based on **viewpoint** (the first, second and third person), which he defines as "*where* the narrator exists within the fabric of the retelling." He relates viewpoint to *distance*, meaning movement from a narrator-centred viewpoint towards an increasingly abstract one. He concludes that time has "a close relationship to narrative distance."

We suggest a simpler temporal frame of reference within a work:

1 *Intermission*: where the author or narrator intervenes in the storytelling to make a comment or provide extra-contextual information.
2 *Progression*: where actions and events run sequentially.
3 **Reduction** and **expansion**: where timeframes are shortened or lengthened.
4 *Abstraction*: where time and event sequencing do not progress logically.

In non-fiction, the flow of information or reasoning usually progresses logically; otherwise, the drift and purpose of the writing would be unclear to readers, resulting in their abandoning the book or having to make extra effort to grasp its meaning.

One particularly relevant contribution made by literary theory to the time factor in literature is a concept called *narratology*, developed by Gérard Genette in *Narrative Discourse* (published in 1972 and translated into English in 1980). Genette takes a structuralist view of narration, which examines the relations between narrative and narrating, and between story and narrating. According to Hans Berten:

The first concerns the way in which the chronological *order* of the events and actions of . . . a novel . . . is presented in the actual story. We can express the relationship between the chronological order and the narrative order in terms that express their relative positions at a given point. The narration may temporarily lag behind the chronological order of events (which is what we find in a *flashback* – although Genette does not use the term), it may be synchronic with events, or it may run ahead of them (when the narrator speculates about the future). It may even present unlikely combinations of these possibilities.

(Hans Berten, *Literary Theory – The Basics*, 2014: 61)

Genette also discusses **duration**, which examines the relationship between the time it takes for an action to take place in the construct of the narration and the time it takes to narrate the event. For practical reasons, narration must be compressed: equal duration would, for obvious reasons, be impractical. He also refers to **frequency** as the number of times an event occurs in real life, as opposed to the numbers of times it is narrated.

The significance of these concepts is that they force translators to position themselves within the text. Translators do not merely read the text and follow the storyline but also attempt to recreate it in another language as closely as the language combination permits, given the linguistic and cultural constraints of both languages. In particular, the narratological technique of the author needs careful consideration: for example, where an event is compressed in the source, it must be equally compressed in the target to achieve any kind of equivalence. This is sometimes easier said than done, if the target language tends to be wordier than the source.

Time is crucial to the structure of novels and plays, to some poetry and to literary translation, given the role it plays in defining the sequence of actions in the storytelling (fiction) or theme development (non-fiction), and therefore merits further analysis and development.

Time (actions/events/occurrences) goes hand in hand with the narrative plot (or "emplotment," as Ricoeur calls it, using Aristotle's concept) in that it provides a vehicle to power the storyline. However, Ricoeur defines *action* as

more than the behaviour of the protagonists that produces the visible changes in their situation or fortune . . . Action in this enlarged sense, also includes the moral transformation of characters . . . their initiation into the complexity of moral and emotional existence . . . and purely internal changes affecting the temporal course of sensations and emotions.

(1985: 10)

Evidence of action configured not only as a physical phenomenon but also as an emotive and psychological one (what Ricoeur calls the "temporal course of moral and emotional existence") can be seen in *Les Liaisons Dangéreuses*, written by Choderlos de Laclos in 1782. Here the passage of time and progression of events is narrated in letters exchanged between the various characters, with the reader effectively "peeping through the keyhole" while the events are taking place, experiencing the feelings expressed and hearing about the schemes or actions planned. The fragmentation into letter episodes, in which the various players lay bare their plans or reveal their desires and intentions, creates a kaleidoscope of timeframes, driving the story towards the inevitable tragic ending in this particular case.

Ricoeur mentions Daniel Defoe as having "recourse to a pseudo-autobiographical form, through imitation of the innumerable diaries, memoires, and genuine autobiographies published at the same time." Moreover, he sees Richardson's novels *Pamela* and *Clarissa* as depicting private experience "with even greater fidelity by using as artificial a device as the exchange of letters, despite its evident disadvantages" (1985: 11). These early forms of fiction clearly show how timeframes can be created and manipulated to shorten or prolong actions or to describe states of mind, while drawing in the reader and propelling the action towards its climax. Ricoeur explored how the concept of time was handled in three literary works: Virginia Woolf's *Mrs Dalloway*, Thomas Mann's *The Magic Mountain* and Proust's *Remembrance of Things Past*. Our focus is specifically translation-based, and we will examine how the time and date of a translation affects the choices the translator makes. Similarly, but perhaps to a lesser extent, these choices are governed by the time and context in which the source text first appeared.

Time is particularly important in historical novels: after *Wolf Hall* by Hilary Mantel won the Booker Prize in 2009, there was much discussion about historical accuracy. James Forrester, writing in *The Guardian* (6 August 2010), wrote,

> The path a historical novel has to tread is clearly beset by dangers. There is an inherent tension in trying to do something new and something old at the same time. One cannot have medieval characters using correct period language because no-one would find the speech readable.

He also said, "too much attention to factual detail is undoubtedly an impediment to literary art."

These considerations hold good for the translation of texts set in a distant period of history but also for those with modern and contemporary settings.

Writers in the French *nouveau roman* movement in the 1950s, such as Michel Butor and Alain Robbe-Grillet, reshaped the novel as a form, experimenting with *circular* as against *linear* narrative. In *La Jalousie*, for example, Robbe-Grillet explored the meaning of reality by playing with shifting timescales and ending the narrative at a similar point to where it began. Butor explored time in *L'emploi du temps* and in *La Modification*, but he also wrote about place in his essays on *Le génie du lieu*. J. B. Priestley was another writer who experimented with different concepts of time in a series of plays, the best known of which is *An Inspector Calls*.

A strong sense of place and the ability to "transport the reader to the dazzling brightness or devastating darkness of the northern countries" is one of the features that may account for the popularity of "Nordic Noir" or "Scandi Noir" literature, according to Karen Sullivan in the October 2017 edition of *The Riveter*, a European Literature Network publication.

Time is, of course, at the very core of science fiction, from its beginnings in the early twentieth century, with H. G. Wells's *The Time Machine* and his *War of the Worlds*, to classic sci-fi by authors like John Wyndham, Isaac Azimov, Ray Bradbury and contemporary writers. Time travel is also a popular theme in children's literature, for example, in C. S. Lewis's classic *The Chronicles of Narnia* series.

However, time does not have to be "realistic" to be intriguing, and if the plot and characters are good, however outlandish the timescales and settings may be, stories that stretch the bounds of time and place will always be a popular form of escape.

> **Pause for thought**: In your view, does fragmenting the plot into episodes or letters, as in some of the works mentioned earlier, make it easier or more difficult to follow the story as a reader? And as a translator?

RELEVANCE OF CONTEXT

As mentioned, we will consider context in two ways: *logistically*, as the situation where something exists or happens and *linguistically*, as the positioning of a lexical or semantic unit within its surrounding discourse. In its relation to time, the logistical function of context is to "frame" an action, event or idea through language and to convey a clearer image by means of supporting information. The context itself may be just a few words, or a more extensive utterance, depending on the writer's intention and needs. For example, it may be sufficient to refer to "the dining room," if reference has been made to this room previously, but in a subsequent reference, it may be necessary to provide more detail in order to generate a clearer image or concept. The provision of context enables the reader to visualise something or someone at a particular stage in the evolution of the work and to create a clearer picture. Context is needed to dispel ambiguity ("in the dining room at the Ritz," rather than "at the Savoy," or "in the dining room" rather than "in the kitchen"), but it may also be necessary to flesh out the concept or image with a full, or at least fuller, description to provide the coordinates the reader needs to navigate the text successfully.

Specific references to places and dates may be omitted, as in some eighteenth- and nineteenth-century literature: in *Les Liaisons Dangéreuses*, Cécile Volanges (who becomes the target of the Vicomte de Valmont's seduction plan) writes to her friend Sophie "aux Ursulines de . . ." (at the Ursuline convent of . . .), and Valmont writes to the Marquise de Merteuil (his confidante) "du Château de . . . ce 9 août 17**" (from the Château of . . ., 9th of August 17–), following the conventions of the time for avoiding specific references. By omitting place names and dates, the author creates environments that appear detached from reality, existing in a kind of limbo or allegorical parallel world. This technique may also give the impression of moral intent (although Laclos claimed this was not his reason for writing the book). Nonetheless, the omissions and use of fictitious names of characters did not prevent certain aristocrats of the period from believing that they were being "tarred with the brush" Laclos was wielding in his depiction of the debauchery of the day. The book successfully evokes the loose morals, indulgence and extravagance of high society in the late eighteenth century by creating a kind of time warp, which cleverly combines context and time. The use of the letter exchange technique is intriguing for both contemporary and present-day readers, though the way readers from different periods relate to the book is influenced by the cultural and moral climate of the **reading time**.

On a practical note, translators could learn from the approach adopted by the biographer Claire Tomalin in her autobiography *A Life of My Own* (Viking, 2017, p. 285). Speaking of the biographer's relationship with the subject and her method of research, she says, "You will have walked in their footsteps and travelled where they travelled." Some years before, the historian Richard Cobb had advised her to do this, recommending that when studying eighteenth-century lives, you should "walk where they walked, if possible, or go on horseback to see the world as they did" (2017: 190). Claire demurred at travelling on horseback and chose to travel by bicycle instead. This aim for authenticity in culture and context is worth considering with respect to translation, though few translators would go to these lengths!

In *Literary Criticism – A Graphic Guide*, the authors aptly ask, "Can the 'words on a page' of a given poem or novel really be held in splendid isolation from the text's historical and cultural reception, or its history of publication and translation?" (Holland and Piero, 2015, Icon Books Ltd., p. 7). Another perspective on the "critical heritage" of a text concerns interpretation. In the context of **historicism** (defined in the book of the same name by Paul Hamilton as "insisting on the prime importance of historical context to the interpretation of texts of all kinds," the author wonders whether historicists "can distinguish between the meaning a piece of writing had for its first audience and a real meaning, unclouded by that original audience's or any subsequent period's ideology" (in *Historicism*, Hamilton, 1996, Routledge: 2). He also points out that "Any historical enterprise inevitably reflects the interests and bias of the period in which it was written" (1996: 3).

Thus, interpretation of a text, in particular for a translator, is a complex process, consisting of the "words on the page" in their specific context, delivered through linguistic signs and the consequent meanings and connections they generate in the translator's mind.

Context has been explored by various prominent philosophers and linguisticians, particularly semioticians. Derrida wondered, "How can a context assure 'correct meanings'?" and "Can context provide meaning with a safe haven from undecidability?" (see: *Introducing Derrida – A Graphic Guide* by Jeff Collins, Icon Books, 2011: 79). By this, he means, can a context always be relied upon to accurately project the image or content intended by the author? There are certain invariables in a context: for example, this volume is a written product, a book, by two authors, who are communicating ideas. That much is clear. Such conventions can be received and processed more or less equally by readers. But when it comes to words that describe a specific action, event, scene or emotion, no amount of detail will conjure up exactly the same image in everyone's mind or the one originally in the author's mind, as each individual brings his or her own life experience to the work in a unique way, as we have mentioned. Even the description of a place likely to be familiar to many people will not generate the exact same picture in every reader's mind. A good example is the following description from *A Legacy of Spies* by John Le Carré (Penguin Modern Classics, 2018), where the protagonist, former spy Peter Guillam, reminisces about the Cold War:

> Berlin safe house K2 lies in the Fasanenstrasse, at No. 28, and is a stately and unlikely survivor of Allied bombing. It is built in the Biedermeier style with a pillared doorway, a bay window and a good back exit leading on to the Uhlandstrasse. Whoever chose it had a taste for imperial nostalgia and an operational eye.
>
> (2018: 110)

As Hans Georg Gadamer suggests in *Philosophical Hermeneutics* (1976), "The work of art would seem almost by definition to be an aesthetic experience; that means, however, that the power of the work of art suddenly tears the person experiencing it out of the context of his life, and yet relates him back to the whole of his existence" (University of California Press, p. 70). If we apply that idea to the preceding example, we might conclude that few people, apart from Berliners, are likely to be familiar with the house mentioned or the two streets, while the reference to the Biedermeier style, prevalent in parts of Europe in the 1830s, may be unfamiliar to some people. Even if these references are familiar, the appearance of the house and streets could have changed since the sixties (when the action is set). However, this does not stop the reader from forming a picture, however vague and fleeting, in his or her own mind of the scene (an "aesthetic experience"). As far as translation is concerned, the context is clearly of paramount importance, particularly where it cannot be "relied upon" as a statement of fact. Derrida considered that the whole matter of translation was a problem and suggested that, in effect, translators have to say, but also not say, what someone has said. The **inferences** drawn by the reader/translator from the text are therefore crucial to the way the information is processed through the reader's or translator's world view, which is, at least to some extent, unconsciously subjective.

Given the inherent subjectivity of the interpretation process, the linguistic context of a lexical or semantic unit through which the writer conveys his or her ideas, and the words chosen, should deliver a message that is clear (unless the language used is intended to be unclear or incoherent, for example, in poetry or to express feelings like perplexity, uncertainty, fear, doubt). However, an utterance in a specific context may be received one way by a speaker of that language yet quite differently by someone else. The potentially arbitrary interpretation of language, even in a very specific context, is what makes reading, understanding and translating a text a challenging activity.

As Paul Hamilton points out in *Historicism* in his discussion of hermeneutics (the art of understanding),

> Hermeneutics is the science of interpretation. It stresses the individuality of each human expression and, against scientific generalizations, claims that we choose between the several meanings any utterance may have in the light of the special circumstances under which it is made. In this way we resolve grammatical ambiguities, appreciating, for example, that commands in one situation are not intended to hold good in another.
>
> (1996: 51)

This is no doubt true to some extent, but it is patently clear to any translator that meaning transcends the formal elements of language and extends to the context (i.e., the "special circumstances") in which it is created, including what the reader or translator may read into the text. We could call this *psychological context*. In colloquial speech in some languages (for example, French and English), an utterance lacking an interrogative pronoun or specific interrogative form (a statement) may also be intended as a question; if an interrogative intonation is used, the listener will receive the utterance as a question.

Political discourse, in particular, contains a number of variables that can affect its reception: for example, a British government minister might promise "a massive injection of cash to support education after Brexit." A person who has voted for the party in government is more likely to believe the promise than someone who supports the opposition, who may well think it is just a cynical ploy to please or appease the public. But even someone who supports the government might harbour doubts about investment on this scale. Such doubts are often reflected in the way journalists relay politicians' words, especially in reported speech.

In our "post-truth" society and the age of social media, the message is often blurred. This issue was highlighted in "Lexicon of a Leader," a recent article by Yelena McCafferty, published in the May–June 2017 issue (pp. 6–7) of the *ITI Bulletin*, a specialist journal for translators and interpreters. The author discussed the difficulties interpreters encounter when rendering Donald Trump's speeches and tweets into Russian and other languages.

Because Donald Trump's use of discourse is very different to the way most politicians speak, we have to ask ourselves whether we can take his words at face value. Does the context in which he utters them throw any light on what he really means?

Derrida is no doubt wise to consider translation as a perilous activity, which is fraught with difficulty: in his opinion, while no text is absolutely translatable, it is not absolutely untranslatable either, so most translations fall somewhere between these two parameters. This idea is further developed in "What Is a Relevant Translation?" (Jacques Derrida and Lawrence Venuti, in *Critical Inquiry* 27, no. 2, Winter, University of Chicago).

The difficulty of producing valid and coherent theories on the use and meaning of language eventually led to the science of **semiotics** (defined by *Oxford Living Dictionaries* as "The study of signs and symbols and their use or interpretation"), which has made a significant contribution to the debate on how language works in context. For example, the semiotician Thomas Sebeok suggested that all semiosis – "an action or process involving the establishment of a relationship between a sign and its object and meaning" (*Collins Online English Dictionary*) "takes places in a significant environment or *Umwelt*" (*Semiotics – A Graphic Guide*, 2012, Icon Books Inc.). By *Umwelt*, Sebeok means

> the part of an environment that an organism "chooses" to inhabit; it is the perceptual or "subjective" universe of the organism. . . . Conversely, the *Umwelt* also shows that it is in itself a sign of the organism, in that it is possible to make inferences about the organism based on an analysis of its environment.
>
> (2012: 126–7)

In 1970, Sebeok developed this theory, suggesting that "In this formulation, the products of human behaviour – linguistic texts, cultures, social institutions – are not so much the result of unfathomable creativity as of a series of limitations or choices of operation" (Cobley & Jansz, 2019, 2012: 129). The limitations are represented by the words themselves, in two ways: the sign (or meaning) of a word or phrase is produced by an individual, who imbues it with meaning; however, the way the meaning of the word or phrase is received and interpreted by the reader will depend on the standard linguistic framework and conventions of that language (grammar, **syntax**, structure), as well as the specific frame of reference (linguistic context) in which it is situated. This binary framework reflects the earlier theory of **semiology**, developed by Ferdinand de Saussure, who identified individual speech acts as *parole*, and the system of differences between signs as *langue*. One shortcoming of this theory is that although *langue* is used by a language community, it is still an abstract system – in essence, an intangible framework waiting to be employed to create tangible communication, or in metaphorical terms, "*Langue* can be thought of as a communal cupboard, housing all the possible different signs which might be pulled out and utilized in the construction of an instance of *parole*" (2012: 15). This metaphor is very apt for translators, who are involved in "ransacking" that cupboard in order to identify exactly what the text is communicating.

Pause for thought: In standard translator training, students are usually provided with a "**translation brief**" (information relevant to the task and function of the target text that simulates information from a work-provider). However, in real life, specific briefs are relatively infrequent. Assess the impact the lack of a brief may have on a) a text describing a tourist resort; b) an advert for beauty products.

Just to put this into context with a real-life practical example, one of the authors once had to translate a set of French publicity materials about a coconut-based beauty product. The texts included lots of highly specific botanical and anthropological details about coconuts and how they were used in the culture of South Sea Islands (one even being to repair fractured skulls). The brief was relatively vague, but the translator was led to believe that the background information would be used in publicity brochures used to launch a new line of beauty treatments. This was long before the advent of the Internet, so the lack of a specific brief meant she had to go to a library to consult botany books together with back issues of *National Geographic*, which provided the more colourful details of the uses islanders made of various parts of the coconut. The relevance to the context of beauty was not entirely clear, but it was certainly a fascinating assignment.

RELEVANCE OF CULTURE

Culture reflects the historical, geographical, linguistic and social setting; extra-contextual circumstances and information; traditions; values; and behaviour.

An important distinction is generally made between material and non-material culture: **material culture** refers to physical objects that people can create and attach meaning to (such as clothes and food). Natural objects, such as wood or stone, are not considered material culture, but how people view them *is* material culture. **Non-material culture** refers to abstract ideas that are not embodied in physical objects. Intangible products created or shared by members of a culture over time are aspects of non-material culture (such as social roles, rules, ethics, beliefs, history and behaviour). In essence, the difference is between what is material and what is symbolic.

With regard to non-material culture, Mireille Gansel's meditation *Translation as Transhumance*, which appeared in an excellent English translation by Ros Schwarz in 2017 (published by Les Fugitives Ltd), gives remarkable insights into the process of poetry translation, in her case from German and Vietnamese into French. Gansel likens the role of the translator in the migration of images and ideas from one language to another to the movement of shepherds guiding their flocks from the mountainside to fresh pastures.

While this distinction between the two forms of culture is not necessarily of crucial importance for the translator, as these concepts are universal, at text level, they play a strategic role in informing the setting of the action, plot or theme, particularly when we consider the role played by non-material cultural items, which may be less immediately recognisable as transmitters of cultural content (for example, beliefs and judgements). The boundaries between material and non-material culture can be blurred, thus challenging common perceptions, as in George Orwell's great classic *Nineteen Eighty-Four* (published in 1949), where everyday items can take on sinister connotations. In the following passage, the protagonist, Winston, lives in a nightmare world where everything is controlled, even thoughts. Here items of non-material culture are extremely uncomfortable:

> It was terribly dangerous to let your thoughts wander when you were in any public place or within range of a telescreen. The smallest thing could give you away. A nervous tic, an unconscious look of anxiety, a habit of muttering to yourself – anything that carried with it the suggestion of abnormality, of having something to hide. In any case, to wear an improper expression on your face (to look incredulous when a victory was announced, for example) was itself a punishable offence. There was even a word for it in Newspeak: *facecrime*, it was called.
>
> (Penguin Classics, 2000: 65)

Here, **denotation** becomes **connotation**; what is normal in one context becomes abnormal and unacceptable in another. By imbuing unexceptional words and phrases with sinister nuances, Orwell creates a frightening new "culture," akin to the visual environment of the British TV cult classic *The Prisoner*.

Many attempts have been made to define culture. In addition to the one given earlier (which reflects what is essentially an anthropological view), Raymond Williams, one of the founders of cultural studies, considered it "the organization of production, the structure of the family, the structure of institutions which express or govern social relationships, the characteristic forms through which members of the society communicate" (in *Introducing Cultural Studies*, Icon Books Ltd., 2010: 5), while Clifford Gertz (Professor of Social Sciences at Princeton University) suggested that culture was simply the collection of stories people tell about themselves. Basically, anything and everything is "culture."

Cultural references may be difficult to transfer between source and target, where a standard one-to-one equivalent form does not exist. Proper nouns can be problematic: the English acronym NATO is also NATO in Italian, but it is OTAN in French. The name of an Italian city may well be translatable in French (e.g., Parma/ Parme; Pisa/Pise) but not in English. Romance languages can easily generate adjectives from place names, but in English, they are usually only available for the main Italian cities (Roman, Neapolitan, Venetian, Milanese). Changing social attitudes also mean that transfers of names from non-European cultures may alter over time: Calcutta has become *Kolkata* and Peking *Beijing* (to reflect the sound of the original language more closely). Not so long ago, the Swiss city now referred to in English as Basel was written *Basle* or even *Bâle*. Utterances containing several proper nouns can also cause headaches, particularly where it would be appropriate to transfer some of the items into the target language but perhaps not others. Anyone who has translated tourist literature will be acquainted with these kinds of challenges. To make matters worse, all sorts of false friends exist: a president may head a company in the USA, but the term is not normally used in the UK for such an office. Political correctness suggests that we use the term chair (or chairperson) instead of chairman in the UK, but CEO (chief executive officer) is an acceptable "genderless" label. The Italian *Presidente del Consiglio* is not the *Presidente della Repubblica* (the former office equates to a prime minister, while the latter to the president of Italy). A professor in a British university is certainly not the same as a *professore* in Italy (who is any teacher, except a primary school one) or a *professeur* in France. In Italy, a *Dottore* is someone with a degree, not necessarily in medicine, while the standard term for a doctor is *medico* (though the form of address for both is *Dottore*).

In *The Travels of Harry: International Marketing and the Translation of J. K. Rowling's Harry Potter Books*, Gillian Lathey reported on a seminar where delegates compared various international editions of the first volume in the Harry Potter series: *Harry Potter and the Philosopher's Stone*. German-speaking delegates felt that the first chapter (translated into German by Klaus Fritz) was "well done overall" but "loses its Britishness." They had in fact been asked beforehand to consider how the translators mediated an essentially British text. Was there evidence of Klingberg's "cultural context adaptation" in the process of translation, and if so, what was its effect? She adds,

> The peculiarities of the English boarding school and associated foodstuffs may well puzzle the child reader in the target culture, and Rowling draws on these traditions with a degree of panache that the translator has to try to match. Even for those of us who have never been Harry Potter fans, the close textual analysis essential to the comparison of translation and original does lead to an appreciation of Rowling's style: the finesse with which she combines a closeness to spoken language, the ironic tone, linguistic creativity, and narrative momentum.
>
> (*The Lion and the Unicorn*, Volume 29, Number 2,
> April 2005, Johns Hopkins University Press)

In many cases, cultural references are so obscure that they would be meaningless to readers from other cultures without some background information being provided. This can be in the form of a **gloss**, which should contain the information that is implicit in the sub-text to the extent that it can be inferred from the source text by the average native speaker. It should not add unnecessary details, however interesting and engrossing the translator finds them. Incorporating such facts would constitute a serious "offence," that of translator intrusion. Of course, it can be difficult to know where the line needs to be drawn.

A job recently completed by one of the authors was the translation of an academic paper by a professor at the Sorbonne to be presented at a colloquium in Germany. For such an international audience, the translator needed to add a lot of background information of which an educated French person would have been aware but German, British and American audiences would not. This included references to Clovis without expanding on facts that most French readers would have learned at school, namely that he was a Merovingian king, whose baptism in 498 CE was considered by French Catholics to represent the origins of the French nation. Other references would have lost much of their socio-political import if left merely as names of organisations, such as the *Manif pour Tous* (the movement that demonstrated against the bill to introduce equal marriage in France). Glossing needs to be performed with a light touch, and later in the book, we will explore examples that demonstrate how to do it effectively. The translator needs to consider what additional information is *essential* to the message because it is part of the subtext. The key question is will the impact of what the writer is saying be reduced if information that is implicit is omitted?

The interaction of culture with time and context is of great significance to the translator, as cultural content also reflects social attitudes and values. In cross-cultural terms, which are naturally important to translators, a difference is made between **monochronic** and **polychronic** time. In the former, a society prefers to concentrate on one task at a time, promptness of execution and completion, and strict planning, whereas the latter term implies a flexible, multi-tasking approach in which relationships are more important than tasks. This distinction frequently leads to sweeping **generalisations** about a people or culture; for example, the Germans and British tend to be seen as pragmatic, task-based individuals, whereas Poles and Italians are considered more family-oriented.

When translating any text, there are cultural matters to consider, which may be specific items like a place name or local custom or intangible concepts like beliefs, traditions and judgements. A further set of challenges concerns decisions on whether to "localise" the target text in order to aid reader comprehension. These challenges will be discussed in Chapter 3.

The main challenges facing the translator concern the translatability or transfer of these items into the target language and any subjective cultural bias or set of assumptions which may influence the translator's attitude and the choice of language. We have referred earlier to the translator's "cultural share" (i.e., his or her world view (*Weltanschauung*) based on experience, interests and beliefs).

This raises a further issue. As a function of their cultural share, translators may find the subject matter of a text for translation to be a hostile environment if it contains matter that they find distressing or unacceptable. One of the authors of this book was offered a detective story to translate involving a group of hunters who went out every day shooting birds and other creatures. To the author, there was nothing unusual in such a scenario: hunting is seen as a traditional, manly pursuit in his culture, while to the translator, graphic details of killing animals for pleasure and sport is abhorrent. In the same way, a translator asked to translate material relating to head-hunters from New Guinea or Jack the Ripper may be equally reluctant to tackle a subject he or she finds unpleasant from a personal cultural perspective. The problem is not only the subject matter but also the length of exposure to the translation of "unpleasant" matter; readers may well gloss over such details if they are interested enough in the story or subject, but the translator's exposure to unpleasantness may affect his or her ability to produce a good translation, in part because of the potential need to carry out research into the subject matter, which he or she may find distressing.

Pause for thought: Can you think of any topic or subject that you would be unwilling to translate? Would you be able to overcome this unwillingness? If so, in what circumstances? How might this affect the quality of your translation? What moral stance should the translator take?

THE CREATIVE STRAND

In *Literary Translation*, Chantal Wright encourages translators to think of themselves as "literary scholars and translating writers" (Routledge, London: 2016). A similar approach was adopted by Ann Pattison for the *Painting with Words* workshop concept she developed to help both students and practising translators enhance their target language writing skills.

In these workshops, translators were encouraged to write in response to various stimuli and introduced to some of the devices that writers use to create the illusion of a third dimension and set up a plausible context to a story. A visual image of a particular setting or period in history is normally limited to two dimensions, but by appealing to your other senses, that is, smell, taste, touch and hearing, it is possible to generate an almost three-dimensional image of a place or time.

Some authors write so instinctively that their work appears to have been touched by magic, but most people need a great deal of practice before they can produce an evocative description. In Albert Camus's novel *The Plague*, a character called Grand is trying to write a novel, but he has been stuck on the first paragraph for years. He has written and rewritten a passage about a woman on a horse in order to find exactly the right words, instead of moving on and revising the opening once the book is finished. The mistake he makes is that he thinks everything has to be perfect from the very first **sentence**. It doesn't. The key is to get something down on paper and then go back to it later, looking at the text with a reader's rather than with a writer's eyes. At this stage, any superfluous material can be deleted or saved as what journalists call **overmatter**, that is, material that might come in useful one day for a different article.

Because translators are, in a way, writers by proxy, the final section of the book includes exercises to help you to get your creative writing muscles working. In this way, you will start to develop your own writing voice, which you ideally need to find before you can truly identify and replicate another writer's voice.

Some of the creative writing exercises in Chapter 4 have been specially designed to introduce you to the concepts of time, context, and culture from a writer's perspective. The prototypes were given a "test drive" first within a writing group and then further developed for a second "test run" in a workshop for professional translators.

CHAPTER 2

Exploring time, context and culture through language

In *The Politics of Writing* (Routledge, 1997, pp. 230–231), Romy Clark and Riz Ivanič introduced the concept of critical language awareness. Their main focus being sociolinguistics, they studied writing practices and the social context in which texts are created and read. They also explored how linguistic features can be used and sometimes exploited to convey a particular type of message, encouraging readers to look more closely at nuances that can be detected in word choices, making a useful distinction between the **context of situation** and the **context of culture**.

Drawing on Halliday's definition, they explain that *context of situation* includes the place, time and people involved. When applied to written language, it concerns the immediate environment of both the act of writing and the act of reading. The important factors they define are the "relation of power" between the participants within such a context and their ideological positions (i.e., their interests, values, beliefs, commitments, allegiances and sense of self-worth).

These authors see the context of culture as having several levels, including national, institutional and global, and they explore the nature of the discourse community within which texts are produced and the dominant conventions within them.

How is this relevant to translation? Well, it is important for translators to be aware of *what the prevailing conventions are* within a particular discourse community. For instance, most people working on academic texts in the social sciences would be aware that a formal tone is required, so contractions such as *don't* are best avoided except in direct quotes and that *do not* should be written out in full. Similarly, they would refrain from using a **phrasal verb** such as *turn up* and would opt for the more formal *appear*.

A written discourse convention taught in high schools in France and in many other European countries is the strategy of elegant variation, that is, of using **synonyms** such as *l'hexagone*, for example, to avoid repeating the words *la France* or *il Bel Paese* and *la penisola* for Italy. Sometimes, this stylistic device can be taken to extremes. In an Italian article on British companies leaving the UK due to fears about Brexit, Frankfurt (a location of choice for some banks) was referred to as the financial hub on the River Main, the city of German skyscrapers, the city where other major financial institutions are based and, last but not least, the metropolis of the Hesse region. When translating into English for an educated readership, this level of detail about Frankfurt is unnecessary and needs toning down; otherwise, the translation will sound too "exotic": essentially, the readers want to know why the companies are leaving and where they are going ("E' Brexodus: ecco dove vanno aziende e banche in fuga dal Regno Unito," Enrico Marro, *Il Sole 24 Ore*, 16 March 2018). This practice is prevalent in the UK too but generally only with the names of politicians and other public figures, who are usually mentioned once and then referred to by their post. But in French texts, it extends to institutions, such as the French national education system, which is widely referred to as *le mammouth* (the mammoth).

Another convention is the use in French and some other Romance languages of the conditional tense to express a theory, an allegation or an assumption that has not yet been substantiated by facts. In English, the convention is to use a verbal form, such as *is alleged to*, *is believed to*, or a prepositional phrase, such as *according to a spokesperson*.

In German, a common discourse convention is the use of the subjunctive to indicate reported speech, something which may escape the attention of less experienced translators. A report on the Fußverkehrskongress (pedestrian conference) in Berlin in October 2018 stated, for example, *Nach Studien sei jede zehnte Autofahrt kürzer als ein Kilometer, und auf Strecken von einigen Hundert Metern sei man zu Fuß von Tür zu Tür häufig am schnellsten.* (According to studies, every tenth car journey is shorter than one kilometre, and on distances of a few hundred metres, you can often get from door to door faster on foot – *Berliner Zeitung* 11.10.18.) In the absence of information that attributes the information to a specific or, in this case, non-specific source ("studies"), you need to "flag up" the reported speech by inserting a "dummy" subject and verb, such as "he said" or "she continued," because an individual's own perception of an event could otherwise be taken to be an established fact or universal truth. Sometimes, this is not necessary and a past tense in English will suffice, but the use of the modal verb *können* (to be able) often creates problems when used in the present subjunctive form *könne*, as *could* is ambiguous. It has the meaning of *might be able* or *was able*. A report in a recent press release stated "*ein fließender Übergang könne gestaltet werden*," and the translation read "a smooth transition *can* be established," using the present tense because the situation being described was ongoing, but the translator added "she said" to make it clear that this was reported speech.

Discourse conventions do not remain static; like language itself, they *change over time*. In a recent discussion with a colleague who translates German correspondence, we compared letter-writing conventions in English and German during World War I in order to determine the best English equivalents for certain set expressions. Age and class appeared to play a part in the terminology or **lexis** used by the English soldiers. Letters preserved in Sutton archives showed Fred Sharp, a middle-class family man in his thirties, signing off with "Your loving boy" when writing to his wife. He generally addressed her in rather formal and precise language, such as "Will you kindly send me a small pillow slip." Another letter-writer,

Jack Widdecombe, a cheeky single man of about nineteen from a lower-middle-class area, used the formal opening "My Dear Mother and Father" when writing to his parents and signed off as "Your affect Son" (*affect* being his own abbreviation for "affectionate"). A middle-aged family man called Sam Currier from a more deprived area wrote to "My Dear Children" and signed off "with love from Daddy." To his wife and family, he wrote "with best love and wishes to you all I remain your ever loving, Sam."

Due to the limited research material available, it was not possible to find direct equivalents in the archive material for the following expressions used in correspondence from German World War I soldiers, but suggested versions were as follows: *Sei herzlichst gegrüßt* – "All my love"; *Grüße auch die Mutter* – "Give Mother my love too"; *Ich grüße und umarme Dich* – "I send you my very best wishes and embrace you." An alternative rendering of the latter, namely "All my love and a big hug," was rejected because the concept of a hug might be thought too modern.

It is important to realise that many authors see discourse conventions as rules that are there to be broken! Most writers try to be original and avoid clichés. After all, they want to sell large numbers of books, so they will often try to flout the rules by creating unusual **collocations** (sets of words used in combination, such as nouns and verbs, nouns and adjectives or verbs and adverbs). Standard English collocations include *to come to a finale*, *to raise a question*, *to gather material*, *to draw a conclusion* and *to address a problem*. The term **cliché** describes an expression that is so overused in everyday language that it has become meaningless, such as "*blue sky thinking*," "*transformational*" and "*can-do culture*." In the 1960s, the expression "*Let's run it up the flagpole and see if anyone salutes it*" was adopted by young executives to suggest putting forward an idea to see if it gained approval, but it finally became a cliché and fell out of use. Not only individual phrases but also whole concepts can become clichéd when it appears that they will not sustain the reader's interest. Following J. K. Rowling's success with her boy wizard, for instance, literary agents were warning new writers against creating Harry Potter clones.

As a translator, you need to remain critically aware and reflect the originality or lack of it in the source text by also employing original expressions or non-standard usage in your target language version. Sometimes academic authors use "scare quotes" to warn the reader that they have coined a new expression or used a jargon term, and this strategy is available to translators, too.

In this chapter, the analytical criteria we will be looking at initially are those that can be used to apply critical awareness to a source text. When comparing a translation with the source text or with other translations, there are other factors to consider. These relate in the main to the strategy that you have adopted. For instance, does the source text try to be as faithful as possible to the original, or is its main concern readability?

To prepare you for text and translation analysis, consider the following questions:

- What is the text about?
- What is it for?
- What type of text is it?
- What message does it convey?
- Who is likely to read it?
- What level of language is required?
- Whose viewpoint is the text presenting?
- If the text is for translation, will it be published? If so, where?

The answers to these questions will involve considering the following features:

- the subject matter or theme of the text;
- its **purpose**;
- the **genre**, text type and context;
- the lexis or vocabulary and style to use;
- the potential readership;
- the **register** or level of language expected; and
- the degree of objectivity with which the message is conveyed.

Of particular relevance here is the distinction that Peter Newmark made between the semantic and communicative approaches to translation (*About Translation* 1991: 10–11). He described **semantic translation** as author-centred, more literal and closer to the source text and **communicative translation**, in contrast, as reader-centred, focusing on making the target text easy to follow. Newmark saw semantic translation as an art and communicative translation as a craft.

In the preceding quotation from the *Berliner Zeitung*, the phrase "according to studies" is a semantic, or literal, rendering, but if you wanted a more natural-sounding translation, you might adopt a communicative approach and say, "Studies indicate that . . .".

In most newspaper articles, the main aim is to impart information, and therefore, a communicative approach is more suitable, but when translating scientific or philosophical theories, a more semantic approach is usual, especially where there is a need to be ultra-precise. For instance, if a specific bird is mentioned in a guidebook for travellers to the Pyrenees, it is important that ornithologists planning a birdwatching trip to that region are not misinformed. In contrast, the reader of a spy novel is more interested in finding out what is going to happen next in the story and is less likely to want to know which particular species of *rapaces* (birds of prey) can be seen flying over the farmhouse where the terrorists are hiding.

In Anna Pasternak Slater's 2010 *Guardian* review of a new translation of Dr Zhivago by Volokhonsky and Pevear, she quotes a few examples of what indicates to us that this team adopted a *semantic* approach. The reviewer describes the result of this as "a kind of Russified English," such as "Pavel had gone to bathe in the river and had taken the horses with him *for a bath*."

In the 1958 translation, which had, she explains, been done at great speed because the author Boris Pasternak had just won the Nobel Prize, Max Hayward and Manya Harari had adopted a very different translation strategy, namely, to read a page of a Russian novel, put it down and then retell it in English. This communicative translation tells the reader:

Pavel had gone off to bathe in the river and had taken the horses with him.

Because this version had been translated in haste, Anna Pasternak Slater tells us that it resulted in a number of omissions, which the new translators had put right.

A further choice that the translator faces when transposing one culture into another is the choice between two strategies, one of which (**foreignization**) aims to retain the exotic flavour of elements in the source text. The converse is **domestication**, which attempts to make foreign concepts accessible to the **target culture**. These divergent approaches were explored by Lawrence Venuti in *The Translator's Invisibility: A History of Translation*, published by Routledge in 1995 (1995: 20).

A prime example of domestication, which resulted in considerable controversy, is quoted by David Bellos in *Is That a Fish in Your Ear?* (2013, London: Penguin Books). He describes how Cornelius Ruyl, a seventeenth-century Dutch trader and linguist who translated Matthew's gospel into Malay decided to solve the problem of cultural gaps by a process of substitution, replacing the source text word for a fig tree, which did not exist in Sumatra, with a banana tree, which did (2013: 178). Bellos goes on to explain that a similar practice was adopted by the Bible translation consultant Eugene Nida in his preference for what he termed dynamic equivalence, in which source text expressions are substituted with phrasing that has roughly the same force in the target culture (2013: 174–175).

Such a strategy is not always the best thing in an exam situation, as the following cautionary tale will illustrate. A very gifted ex-student once confessed rather ruefully that he had just ruined his chances in a professional translation paper because he had substituted Nicolas Sarkozy with Gordon Brown (both then held similar ministerial posts in their respective governments). In the heat of the examination room, domestication had seemed a good idea, but as soon as he had put his pen down, the candidate realised that within the context of French politics, the use of a target culture equivalent would be at least confusing and at worst directly misleading for the English reader.

The strategy that you adopt to make the source language culture accessible to the target culture may well depend not only on the context but also on what Bellos refers to as the "vertical axis of translation relations." His premise is that acts of translation "typically exploit and support an asymmetrical relationship between source and target tongues." He believes that translation choices depend on whether the translator is working "UP" or "DOWN." He says, "Translation UP is towards a language of greater prestige than the source," such as from the languages of Central Asia into Russian in the days of the USSR. Such prestige can be due to ancient tradition, wider readership, conquest by a powerful nation, greater economic power or the religious importance of writings in the target language.

Translation DOWN is defined by Bellos as being towards a "vernacular with a smaller audience than the source, or towards one with less cultural, economic, or religious prestige, or one not used as a vehicular tongue." As an example of this, he refers to translation from German into Hungarian in the days of the Austro-Hungarian empire (2013: 171–172).

Whether or not you think the descriptors that Bellos uses are appropriate, he makes an interesting observation: "translations towards the more general and more prestigious tongue are characteristically highly adaptive, erasing most of the traces of the text's foreign origin." However, translations into a language with a smaller audience "tend to leave a visible residue of the source, because in those circumstances foreignness itself carries prestige" (2013: 173).

The idea that some authors see a foreign cultural backdrop as carrying prestige is demonstrated by the way authors like Guillaume Musso and Marc Levy often set their novels at least partly in the US and occasionally in the UK. Musso's *L'appel de l'ange* alternates between San Francisco and Paris, while much of the action in *Et Après* takes place in New York, and *Central Park* moves between New York, Paris and Dublin. Marc Levy's *Et si c'était vrai* is set in San Francisco and *L'étrange voyage de Monsieur Daldry* describes a journey from London to Istanbul.

In *Making the "Unstageable" Stageable: English Rewritings of Chekhov's First Play*, Stuart Young writes,

> it is fitting that the more recent English adaptations of the plays are by three prominent playwrights: *Wild Honey* by Michael Frayn, *Piano* by Trevor Griffiths, and *Platonov* by David Hare. Although he presumes to do no more than "merely" translate Chekhov's four major plays (Introduction, *Three Sisters*), Frayn candidly admits to treating *Untitled Play* "as if it were a rough draft of one of my own plays" (Introduction, *Wild Honey*). . . . As a consequence of Frayn's choices regarding style, characterization, and theme in adapting *Untitled Play*, *Wild Honey* exemplifies the strategy, common among translators for the English stage, of naturalizing or domesticating the foreign.
>
> (Source: *Modern drama* ISSN: 0026-7694 Date: 01/10/2009 Volume: 52 Issue: 3 Pages: 325–350)

Pause for thought: Do you translate out of a language of limited diffusion into one with a wider audience or in the opposite direction? Or do you work mainly between two languages of equally wide diffusion? How does this affect the strategies that you choose to adopt? What are the implications?

SUBJECT MATTER/THEME

Before starting work on a translation, you need to have a clear idea of the main theme and, in a work of fiction, of the plot. In this book, we have also included extracts from non-fiction works that we have worked on in a professional context and which relate to art, culture and the history of ideas. In non-fiction, it is important to have a clear overview of the argument and of the direction in which it is heading. One way to sum up the theme of a book or article before attempting to translate it is to borrow a concept from the film industry and write a logline.

A **logline** or strap-line is a jargon term used by scriptwriters who want to pitch their ideas to a potential director or film company. To maximise their chance of getting a contract, they try to sum up the plot in a single sentence. This needs to encapsulate the story in very few words, using *active* rather than *passive* verbs, and show why an idea could have universal emotional appeal. Using generic terms so as to convey universal emotions and scenarios that anyone might experience, the logline sets out the main protagonist/s, the goal that drives them and the antagonist who places obstacles in their path. Novelists and playwrights have found this a useful exercise, too, because it helps them to remain focused on the main theme and avoid writing themselves into a corner. The advantage of this technique for translators is that it helps you to develop clear thinking skills so that you can focus on the key aspects of the source text and identify the basic underlying theme, particularly when a particular passage is written from a new character's viewpoint. Loglines will be explored in greater detail in Chapter 4.

In *Teach Yourself Screenwriting*, published by Hodder & Stoughton in 1996, Raymond Frensham defines theme with regard to screen plays as "that universal statement about the human condition you, the writer, want to make, those ideas or words you want your audience to take away with them at the end to help them live fuller, happier, better, more rounded lives" (1996: 50–51).

Particularly relevant to the concept of the theme of a literary text is what Orhan Pamuk calls "its secret center," its core and real subject, namely, "the intuition, thought, or knowledge that inspires the work" (2016: 155). He stresses that this inspiration may "change direction and shape" as a novel evolves, and the reader's idea of it may change in the course of reading. In the context of the present book, we can substitute "the reader" with "the translator."

A good example of literature that straddles two themes – literature and music – is the composer Francis Poulenc's *Journal de mes melodies* (Diary of My Songs), originally published in Paris in 1964. As Graham Johnson remarks in the *Introduction* to the parallel text in French and English (published in 1989, with the translation by Winifred Radford (1985) for Victor Gollancz Ltd), "Poulenc belonged to that small group of composers who were able to leave important clues to their musical style by non-musical means" (1989: 14). He emphasises the connection between literature and music with the comment, "This Journal is perhaps the most unusual part of the Poulenc legacy, for in words rather than music it suggests the poetic, idiosyncratic, unpredictable workings of a great composer's mind and heart." The following entry, with its translation, expresses his ability to appraise a musical performance (mind) but also a very emotive reaction (heart).

Avril 45	*April 1945*
Je reprends ce Journal par mauvaise humeur. Je l'ai commencé d'ailleurs dans des circonstances analogues. Hier récital de Mme X qui chante avec intelligence, mais avec un minimum de voix. Une pianiste impeccable mais d'une *avarice* sordide quant à la pédale, l'accompagnait. Il paraît que c'était très bien. Je suis sorti ivre de colère de chez Gaveau. Je me fous des chanteuses intelligentes. Il me faut *du chant* avec une bonne sauce de pédale (le beurre, quoi!) sans cela ma musique en crève.	I am resuming this diary in a bad mood. I began it, moreover, in similar circumstances. Yesterday a recital by Mme X who sings with intelligence but a minimum of voice. The accompanist was impeccable, but she was terribly mean when it came to using the pedal. It was a success, it seems. I left the Salle Gaveau in a fury. I detest intelligent singers. I like to hear some *singing* with a good sauce of pedal (the butter!), without which my music is destroyed.

Pause for thought: The preceding translation is around thirty years old. If you feel the language is a little "dated" or the translation too literal, how might you improve on the English? You do not need to know French to perform this task, but if you do translate from French into English, why not have a go at translating it yourselves? Or do you consider, like Vladimir Nabokov, that the task of a translator is "to reproduce with absolute exactitude the whole text, and nothing but the text" (quoted in *The Oxford Guide to Literature in English Translation*, 2000, ed. Peter France, OUP p. 5)?

PURPOSE

The theme of a text is closely related to its purpose. In *Thinking English Translation* (2018: 13) Cragie and Pattison, Routledge: London), we discussed the concept of **Skopos Theory** when considering the intended purpose of the target text or TT (that is, of the translation). In the present volume, we shall be looking more closely at literary and academic source texts, exploring whether and when the purpose of the target text should differ from that of the source text. For instance, should a polemic by a potentially dangerous politician be rendered such as to win support, or should you try to reveal the implicit morally suspect message in your translation and highlight the hazards this idea represents to the world?

Let us first consider the author's purpose in creating a text. Orhan Pamuk says (2016: 68) that one of the strongest "initial urges" he feels when writing a novel is

> to make sure that I can see in words some of the topics and themes, to explore an aspect of life that has never before been depicted and to be the first to put into words the feelings, thoughts and circumstances that people who live in the same universe as me are experiencing!

He sees the art of the novel as showing the world "the way the protagonists perceive it, with all of their senses" and experiencing its landscape from within (*ibid:* 76).

The purpose of a translation will usually depend on the brief provided by the client. Some academic and scientific texts are translated in order to provide a researcher with vital information that would not otherwise be accessible to someone without a good knowledge of the source language. Some years ago, one of the authors of this book was asked to provide a translation of a German research paper published during World War I, which would "turn the whole of physiology on its head," or so the client claimed. (She never did discover whether it did do this.) In other cases, academics may need the services of a translator to help them publish their findings in an international forum. More often, however, the primary purpose of translation is to share good or ground-breaking writing with a wider audience. This raises some interesting and sometimes controversial issues when it comes to translations of works by very well-known writers.

For example, an article in *the ITI Bulletin* ("Visions and revisions," November-December 2018) featured three literary translators, who were specifically asked why texts that have been translated time and again over the years should be re-translated. The answers were intriguing: Josephine Balmer (on her translation of Sappho's poetry) remarks that "the translation is what moves the text on. . . . It's not monolithic; it's a stage in the text's history." Ros Schwartz (on re-translating St Exupéry's *The Little Prince*) mentions that translations today "aim to arouse the response in the reader that the source text arouses in the original language," pointing out that translators today can be more accurate, given greater research possibilities. On translating *Anna Karenina*, Rosamund Bartlett favours "a timeless language, but inevitably translations are of their time." For instance, she mentions that the word *dacha* can now be used as it is "part of the everyday English language." The various stakeholders in the process have different reasons for re-translating a literary text (publisher, translator and possibly author), but essentially, the text itself is deemed worthy of being "dusted down" after previous translations (often considered to be old-fashioned or literal or to contain errors in interpretation), improved on and made accessible to a wider audience. An interesting point, raising the issues of both translation within the twenty-first-century context and the needs of the target reader is made by Ros Schwartz:

> many translators in the past didn't have the kind of ethos or discourse about what they were doing. I think that translators are now discussing what we are doing, and who we are doing it for, even if we may have very different answers.

Pause for thought: Is there a translated literary text that you think is out-of-date or too literal in your language combination? If you were commissioned to retranslate it, what would your approach be? Would you look at previous translations and improve them? Or would you work without consulting previous translations? What are the advantages and disadvantages of these two approaches?

FORM

Here, what we mean by form is the physical layout of the work, which will vary according to the genre and where it falls within the genre. Researchers working on archive material from World War I or World War II may even ask you to translate correspondence that is handwritten. This can be a problem if the documents in question were written at a time when a now obsolete form of handwritten script was used, such as the German Gothic script. In order to decipher some of the abbreviations in application forms filled in by Viennese Jews applying for financial support to help them get out of Austria, one of the present authors had to enlist the help of a German friend who had learnt to use the script at school.

Another type of literature where form is particularly important is poetry. Should the translator attempt to create rhyme or assonance where it exists in the source or focus on conveying the message? To attempt to create rhyme or assonance may well result in an artificial or contrived effect of language, where it is "straitjacketed" to fit the rhyming constraints. One of the authors remembers only too well being asked to translate a sonnet on the wonders of a pasta product, which was a bridge too far!

On a more sombre note, a World War I poem by Guillaume Apollinaire (1915), *L'adieu du cavalier*, recently translated into English by Ian Higgins, is evidence of the translator's ability to overcome the challenges of rhyme and produce a translation that is not only accurate but also a poem in its own right, encapsulating the intense irony of war.

L'adieu du cavalier	*Horseman's Farewell*
Ah Dieu! que la guerre est jolie	God yes! war's a lovely thing
Avec ses chants ses longs loisirs	With all the songs the lazy days
Cette bague je l'ai polie	How I've rubbed and buffed this ring
Le vent se mêle à vos soupirs	I hear you sighing in the breeze
Adieu! voici le boute-selle	God bless! there's the call to go
Il disparut dans un tournant	He mounted turned off past the gate
Et mourut là-bas tandis qu'elle	Arrived and died while she at home
Riait au destin surprenant.	Sat smiling at the quirks of fate.

Pause for thought: Find a short poem in your source language with rhyming lines. Think about how you would approach the translation in your target language. How feasible would it be to attempt to replicate the rhyming lines?

GENRE

In this book, the question of genre is of particular relevance. There are some specific genres (or **text-types**) where there is a focus on time, such as historical novels and science fiction. A more recent popular phenomenon is the time-slip novel. Key examples of this genre are Kate Mosse's books *Labyrinth*, *Sepulchre* and *Citadel*, which are relevant to us because they take place in one geographical context, the area around Carcassonne, and the action and the characters slip back in time from the present day to a period several centuries in the past. Her 2018 novel *The Burning Chambers* is the first of a series of four set at the time of the Wars of Religion in France. She explains, "All my historical fiction is inspired by landscape and the relationship between history, storytelling and place" (Source: www.womensprize forfiction.co.uk/reading-room/find-your-next-read/qa-kate-mosse-new-novel).

J. K. Rowling's Harry Potter novels are a prime example of the innovative use of timeframes in fantasy literature for children. The idea of a world parallel to our own is nothing new (for example, C. S. Lewis's *The Chronicles of Narnia* series), nor is that of a separate world (Tolkien's *The Lord of the Rings*) or of our world invaded by aliens (H. G. Wells's *The War of the Worlds* and John Wyndham's *The Midwich Cuckoos*). In all these books, parallel worlds or cultures are created, and time is manipulated to suit the plot. These books have been widely translated, and the cultural and time-related challenges provide interesting material for analysis.

A relatively new genre that is very much context-based is urban fantasy. In *Rivers of London*, the first book in his series of police procedurals in which a probationary constable and an inspector both have magical powers, Ben Aaronovitch describes London locations in considerable geographical detail, using them to help you to suspend your disbelief *and* accept the concept of the *genii locorum* or gods and spirits of place. This was a challenge, even within the fantasy genre, because the tributaries of the Thames, both past and present, are personified as the offspring of Father and Mother Thames! Yet by the penultimate chapter, the author has wrought enough magic to transport the reader back through the ages in Drury Lane to the time when Roman legionaries were encamped nearby. The book has been translated into a number of languages, including French, German, Italian, Spanish, Hungarian, Czech and Japanese. In the Vienna-based newspaper *Die Presse*, the reviewer describes it as a *Geisterbahnfahrt* (a ghost-train ride) (Source: https://diepresse.com/home/kultur/literatur/725749/Ben-Aaronovitch_Geisterbahn-durch-London).

Pause for thought: In your opinion, what are the main challenges in translating children's fantasy literature? How important is the target age group of the readers (bearing in mind that the Harry Potter stories, for example, are very popular with adult readers)?

TIME

A good example of the complexity of timeframes surrounding a literary work can be seen in *The Three Musketeers*, Alexandre Dumas's famous French *roman feuilleton*. The book was first published in 1842, but the complex network of timeframes starts much further back in time – from the seventeenth-century source material used by the author. However, not content with historical accuracy, Dumas weaves a web of fact and fiction using various sources and his imagination. There have been different translations of the book down the years, starting from early translations in America and in England published in 1846, but new translations continued to appear, reflecting various reworkings of the original French text. The earliest source dates back to work by the seventeenth-century novelist Courtilz de Sandras, in particular his *Mémoires de d'Artagnan*, which contains various themes and characters reworked by Dumas. Lord Sudley produced a translation of *The Three Musketeers* in 1952 for Penguin and in his introduction aptly remarks, "it is interesting to establish how much in the novel is actual historical fact and how much fiction" (*The Three Musketeers*, Penguin Books, 1982: 15). Some of Dumas's characters existed in real life, but they had virtually nothing in common with their fictional counterparts. To complicate matters further, as Sudley points out, "The fact that there are three authentic French texts of *The Three Musketeers* with wide discrepancies between them is likely to expose any translator to charges of inaccuracy" (1982: 23). Dumas did not attempt to make his characters talk as they would have in seventeenth-century France but as in his own day. Sudley comments, "Recurrent new translations are, therefore, both justifiable and necessary, in order to keep this immortal work permanently up to date." His translation was still being used by Penguin as late as 1982. However, the Oxford World Classics edition of 1998 of this work uses a nineteenth-century translation by William Barrow, "as the earliest and most pungent of the half-dozen or so English translations which have been made" (Introduction to *The Three Musketeers*, Oxford World's Classics, 1998: xxii). The existence of reworkings of the original French text and translations of the three versions done at different times already creates a complex temporal framework, even without the "internal" timeframes in the book.

We will explore issues of language later, but a comparison of a short passage from the two translations mentioned shows how archaic the second version sounds compared to the first one. The passage is from the beginning of the book and sets the scene in the small town of Meung, in 1625, where the townspeople have gathered excitedly in the High Street.

> At that time panics were frequent and few days passed without one town or another recording in its archives some event of this kind. Noblemen were at war with one another; the King was at war with the Cardinal; Spain was at war with the King. And besides these public and private wars there were other elements which kept the French countryside in a state of almost perpetual unrest, namely thieves, beggars, Huguenots, and rabble of all sorts. And so, from sheer force of habit, on this bright April morning, hearing an uproar and seeing neither the red and yellow standard of Spain nor the Duc de Richelieu's livery, the citizens rushed in a body to the Jolly Miller Inn.
> (1952 Translation by Lord Sudley for Penguin)

> At that period alarms were frequent, and few days passed without some bourg or other registering in its archives an event of this description. There were the nobles, who made war on each other; there was the king, who made war on the cardinal; there was the Spaniard, who made war on the king; then, besides these wars, concealed or overt, secret or public, there were bandits, mendicants, Huguenots, the wolves and the lacqueys. . . . From this custom, therefore, it arose, that on the aforesaid first Monday in the month of April, 1625, the burghers, hearing a noise, and seeing neither the yellow and red flag nor the livery of the Duke of Richelieu, rushed towards the inn of the Jolly Miller.
> (1846 translation by William Barrow for Park Benjamin)

Pause for thought: Which of the two versions do you find evokes the period more effectively? How is this effect achieved? Try producing a version of the passage in contemporary English; then compare it with the two versions reproduced here.

A similar time-lapse situation from the language perspective occurs in Alessando Manzoni's *The Betrothed* (*I promessi sposi*), where the author is writing in the nineteenth century about events taking place in the seventeenth century. There are several analogies that can be drawn between the two works: first, both reference certain historical events and characters; second, both set their story in the seventeenth century (Manzoni was particularly interested in this period of history); third, both books went through several versions before the final publication; fourth, both have been translated at various times since first publication, after the first or subsequent editions. Moreover, in terms of language, Manzoni "did not put pseudo-archaic dialogue into the mouths of his characters but made them speak the colloquial Italian of his own day, without anachronisms" (Introduction to the 1972 translation by Bruce Penman, *The Betrothed*, Penguin Modern Classics, 26th reprint, p. 13). However, with regard to the translations, Penman comments that they all

> leave something to be desired in method, or accuracy, or both. . . . Some of them have been extensively and badly cut, or use pseudo-archaic jargon for the dialogue – falling into the very trap that the original was the first to avoid.
>
> (1972: 13)

He also points out that there are "a surprising number of mistakes of inter-pretation. It is also sometimes too literal, with extensive passages in the historic present – a device which never sounds right in modern English" (*ibid:* 13). As Pen-man was writing these comments back in 1972, he could not have foreseen that the historic present would become popular as a narrative tense many years later. Certainly, adopting a pseudo-archaic target language would not only be difficult to achieve but would also require a very in-depth knowledge of the language and register in question in order to sound convincing. It is quite common for authors (and translators) to use some archaisms in lexis and register, to create a "period effect."

A good example of how language can be manipulated to suit a specific time or context can be found in Oscar Wilde's play *Salomé*, which he wrote in French in 1892. It was edited, purely from the point of view of language, by two French revis-ers. Lord Alfred Douglas produced a translation of the play in English, of which Wilde was a scathing critic, remarking that Douglas's translation was unworthy of himself and of the work. The Folio publication of 1957 provided a new transla-tion by Vyvyan Holland (Wilde's son) after various "mistranslations" of the French. Interestingly, Holland singles out for special linguistic treatment the character Iokanaan (John the Baptist), "who would be expected to speak in a Biblical way, particularly as some of his utterances are taken from the Scriptures." He seeks to improve on the translation which, by then, was over sixty years old, by adapting "the speech of each of the characters according to his or her personality" (Foreword, *Salomé*, 1957, Folio Society). Holland's characterisation intent is very clear from his archaizing use of language: "Where is she who hath given herself to the Assyrian captains, whose loins are girt with baldricks and wear diadems of divers colours on their heads?" (1957: 24). The archaizing language helps to project a much stronger persona on the audience compared to the language used by the other characters (though with slight variations to distinguish their traits).

Another example of archaizing language can be seen in the work of author and translator Charles Kenneth Scott Moncrieff (1889–1931), who is possibly best known for his translations of Proust. He also translated the medieval poem *Le Chanson de Roland*, to great acclaim. G. K. Chesterton (quoted in Jean Find-lay's excellent biography of C. K. Scott Moncrieff) spoke of the "abnegation of the translator, who is himself a very brilliant and individual writer, in having translated the *Song of Roland*. It would have been easy for a man of his poetic gift to make out of it a modern poem." This he did not do, and Chesterton admired "the literalism that allowed the old text to speak with its own voice, to proclaim its own values," in the words of translation scholar Peter France (Findlay, J. *Chasing Lost Time – The Life of C.K. Scott Moncrieff: Soldier, Spy and Translator*, 2015, Vintage: 175–176). Scott Moncrieff was particularly interested in retaining the assonance and consonance of the original, as these few lines show:

> Li reis Marsilie esteit en Sarraguce.
> Alez en est en un verger suz l'umbre;
> Sur un perrun de marbre bloi se culchet,
> Envirun lui plus de vint milie humes.

> King Marsilies he lay in Sarraguce,
> Went he his way into an orchard cool;
> There on his throne he sate, of marble blue,
> Round him his men, full twenty thousand, stood.
> (2015: 146)

Looking at cultural rather than linguistic ways of evoking different times, the production of Bertold Brecht's *Mother Courage and Her Children* at the Southwark Playhouse in London in November–December 2017 provided a prime example of how a drama set many centuries ago can still convey a universal theme. The play, which used universal rather than archaic language, was described as the "greatest anti-war play of all time." It was written in 1939 when Brecht had left the Third Reich and gone into exile in Sweden. It is ostensibly a chronicle of the Thirty Years War, a time (1618–1648) that the translator, Tony Kushner, defines in his introduction as

> one of the many transitional historical moments when the medieval is yielding to the mercantile (a process arguably still incomplete). In *Courage*, a premodern, peasant Christianity is set against the onslaught of the modern, the vehicle for which is the war.
> (Tony Kushner 2009, Methuen Drama: London)

CONTEXT

Douglas Robinson, in his essay "The Limits of Translation" in *The Oxford Guide to Literature in English Translation* (2000), comments that "the limits of translation are never stable. They are defined pragmatically . . . depending on what scale one is employing, under what constraints, for what audience, to what purpose." He aligns the idea of *constraints* with context, in that "those limits depend so utterly on contextual and perspectival factors like who, when, how or why" (2000: 19).

Considering context as a framework, albeit a shifting one consisting of a set of constraints, creates the environment in which the translator is obliged, but also enabled, to make linguistic and cultural choices. However, how those choices are made will also depend on the many variables arising from the translator's perceptions, understanding of and empathy with the text.

As we have already mentioned, context is linked to time as much as to culture. Unless the setting of a literary work is deliberately abstract, vague or impersonal, the author needs to build a picture (referential framework) to situate the event or action consisting of various coordinates: a timeframe, a setting (physical or psychological) and the characters. A context may be fragmented, kaleidoscopically, into different frames, running forwards or backwards, for example, following the (sometimes erratic) thought processes of the narrator or of a character; it is often a mixture of place, time and emotions, where one scene, idea or thought flows into another. Fiction with a historical bias usually features strong contextualisation, as the reader may have little familiarity with the period in question or may need to possess specific information in order to follow the storyline, or simply to make it more "realistic." In modern and contemporary novels set in a historical context, fact and fiction are frequently blended into "**faction**," a formula that enables the author to use a specific historical timeframe and setting, but one in which characters and events are manipulated for dramatic effect. However, as we have seen with Dumas and Manzoni, faction is not a new concept. It is also popular in visual media, such as film and works for television. However, any discrepancies in historical accuracy can cause ridicule, for example, in blockbusters from the fifties where Alexander the Great or Ben Hur is wearing a wristwatch or where the language does not match the context (for example, the occasional word or phrase that is "untimely" in a drama set in the sixties, as it is a popular utterance today but was not current in the sixties). A more recent example is the reference to "Cumbria" in the televised period drama *Gentleman Jack*, set in the nineteenth century, despite the fact that the designation Cumbria was not in use at the time, having been introduced in 1974.

When considering the setting of a source text, it is not just the geographical and historical backdrop that needs to be analysed but also the whole culture prevalent in the world that the author creates in his or her story. Raymond Frensham (1996: 54) advises aspiring screenwriters to ask themselves what kind of world they have created. It may be a realistic, exotic or fantasy world. He suggests they think about this world's power structures, rituals, ethics and social structure, its climate and its emotional and spiritual life. You, as a translator, will feel better equipped to "get under the skin" of your source text if you try to analyse these factors too.

Pause for thought: The following text is a translation from *Tornare nelle Murge* (Return to Le Murge, an area covering parts of Basilicata in southern Italy) by Carlo Castellaneta, published in 1990 in the magazine *Stagioni* *d'Italia*, Vol 2, Electa Napoli Srl. How does the passage create a setting within a setting? Sometimes contexts are complex, because of the time-frames described or suggested. This passage is from the beginning of the story.

> Now the road sloped down very sharply, after the last bend in the olive grove, and the valley opened up ahead through the windscreen, as if served up on two open hands. Two open hands, mused the man at the wheel. He braked once, then again, and finally came to rest at the side of the road. He had lost count how many hundreds of miles he had driven since the day he set out. The village was still some distance away, but it was those colours, or perhaps simply the dazzling midday glare that made him stop, like someone on the way to an important meeting who takes a moment to collect his thoughts. Occasionally other cars whizzed past, but in the silence between one car and the next there was a kind of thrill in the air, a tremendous vibration that seemed to shake the whole area. The last time he had driven along these roads was thirty-five years ago, on his honeymoon, when he wanted to show Silvia what Le Murge was like, then off they dashed in the Fiat Seicento to Brindisi at top speed so as not to miss the ferry for Patras.
>
> Can you feel nostalgia for a place that forced you to leave it? His father had moved up North with the family when he was just a boy. There were flies behind the curtains, so many they could hardly move, dazed by the heat too, and it was easy to squash them on the window pane with your fingers.
>
> (For the Italian source text, see Appendix, p. 131)

CULTURE

The Castellaneta passage is a good example of how culture interacts with time and context (naturally, in both source and target). The overt cultural references are Le Murge, a valley, a village, Silvia, the Fiat Seicento, up North, Brindisi and Patras, but they are just the tip of the iceberg. Some of these references will be known to the reader or translator, while others are vague (Which village? Where up north?). References such as "olive grove" and "dazzling midday glare" reinforce the image of a hot climate and are more effective than merely referring to "heat." Then there is a culture related to cars and driving; "honeymoon" is a socio-cultural concept, and there are allusions to habitual behaviour, such as taking a break to order one's thoughts or squashing flies on the window. (Does the author see this as typical of boys? Is there any condemnation implied by including this reference, or is it just an example of what the narrator remembers?) Cultural references, whether overt or covert, are frequently challenging for translators, particularly where the cultural assumptions of the source text are not overt, or are only partial, for the **target readership**. Where there is a cultural gap that could result in a loss in translation, there is sometimes a temptation to "embellish" the target text (TT) in order to provide some contextualisation to support the assumed knowledge deficit of the reader. However, this is a risky strategy at the best of times and may result in a text edit rather than a translation.

On the importance of integrating culture into the translation process and making it relevant, in *Translation as Communication across Languages and Cultures*, Juliane House remarks that "In recent decades a major shift in translation studies has occurred away from text – and linguistically-oriented approaches to socially and culturally oriented ones." She points out that there is now a greater emphasis on "translating as a cultural procedure, touching upon issues such as race, class, gender, minority status, ideology and ethics, giving them a central place in analyses of translational phenomena" (Routledge, 2016: 7), concluding that "one does not translate languages but cultures" and asking the question "How does culture affect the construction of meanings in a certain context?" (2016: 32).

While we may consider culture in some respects as a "real thing," House (quoting Gerd Baumannn) comments that culture is a "mental category," which is "an abstract and purely analytical notion. It does not cause behaviour, but summarizes an abstraction from it, and is thus neither normative nor prescriptive" (2016: 35). The episode of the squashed flies in the Castellaneta text is a good example of this idea. It was something that boys typically did: there is no implied censure in the text; it is a form of behaviour, reflecting a moment in time, in a specific cultural context. Ultimately, culture is nothing more (or less) than a recognised pattern of behaviour in a specific social context, rather than individual actions. As far as translation is concerned, it is the correspondence (or, more often, the lack of it) between the source and target cultures that generates the translation challenges. House refers to "linguistic-cultural relativity" in this regard, stressing that "it is knowledge of the application linguistic units have in particular situational and social contexts which makes translation possible." She defines "application" as the relationship "between an expression and the cultural situation in which it is used, its pragmatic meaning" (2016: 48–49).

The concept of "application" is relevant to the potential target readership of the translation if it is to have pragmatic meaning. To give an example, in a French text translated into English for an art exhibition in a New York art gallery, reference is made to an abstract art form called *Tachisme*, from the French word *tache* meaning stain or mark. Research showed that Tachisme is also used in English, but would the target audience understand the term without any gloss or explanation? The text itself does not explain the term. The solution in this case was to send the client a gloss and leave it up to the gallery to decide whether or not to include it in the English version. Assumptions about target audience knowledge can be very difficult to make. Providing too little information can cause a **cognitive**

deficit, while excessive glossing may appear patronising and unnecessary. There-fore, translation decisions are not based solely on text and context but also on the (assumed) cultural knowledge of the target audience. In this case, the audience would typically include "art buffs" but presumably also people simply interested in art, without any in-depth knowledge of art movements and specialist terms.

The issue of pragmatic equivalence is the key to translatability, though as we have seen, cultural references are often more a question of successfully transfer-ring or transposing a phrase and the meaning and implications it embodies in a specific context, rather than translatability as such. While much general equivalence exists between languages in terms of concepts (universality), the same cannot be said of cultural phenomena, where source and target cultures may not share knowl-edge or experience of the phenomenon or phenomena referred to. The range of strategies available to tackle cultural challenges is potentially wider where cultural features predominate in the text. Such items can be translated (a standard transla-tion may exist if it is a common reference, such as an international institution) or described (using a gloss, a footnote or a brief expansion in context) or left in the source language (possibly accompanied by a "transparent" translation) or compen-sated for in some other way. The Internet, while an essential research tool, can also be confusing: the name of an institution might be "translated" into the target language one way on the institution's website (which may or may not "sound right" to a native speaker) or various translations of it (of differing quality) may be found across the Internet. Translators then become editors, in a sense, choosing the form that they think sounds best. For example, names of European universities often have an English translation on their website, which projects an image of an interna-tional, research-oriented organisation. The same may apply to names of museums and galleries, though the institutions themselves usually prefer to keep the title of the institution in the original language. Problems can arise, for example, with a list of museums where exhibitions of an artist have been held, in different languages and venues. A zealous translator who tries to localise all museum or gallery names into the target language could end up with a hybrid and curious list. Consulting the client in advance on such matters is undoubtedly the best course of action.

Pause for thought: Find a text in your source language advertising a forth-coming art exhibition which contains various cultural challenges; set yourself a brief and a target readership and then translate the text into your target language, noting how you approached the cultural and linguistic challenges.

LANGUAGE: LEXIS AND REGISTER

The writer may well have made a deliberate choice of lexis, which in a novel or play may vary from one character to another. In *The Roughs of the Wrythe*, a World

War I play based on real local people who lived in a Surrey village at that time, the dialogue written for the working-class characters contains deliberate grammatical errors. This strategy was adopted in order to replicate the **social register**, whereas the pub landlord, a more educated man who was once a theatre manager, uses more pretentious language. When another character, Willie, says, "I were that proud," Fred corrects him with "Was, dear boy, was."

Writers often use language in this way as an effective shortcut to define a character. For instance, the reader will know that someone who uses obscure words derived from Latin or Greek and talks of *world hegemony* is likely to be a historian, or a social scientist. In the long-running UK radio series *The Archers*, Jim Lloyd, a retired academic, adopts a far more formal **mode of discourse** than his friend Joe Grundy, who used to be a tenant farmer and, rumour has it, a poacher.

Descriptive passages in texts can also be demanding in terms of translation. Envisaging the scene described by the author, through two languages at the same time, with differences in language and culture, raises particular visualisation challenges. These are all too evident in the following passage from Jean Cocteau's *Les enfants terribles* (first published in 1929), in which he paints a picture of a snowy day in Paris:

> Les élèves qui se rendaient en classe avaient déjà gâché, mâché, tassé, arraché de glissades le sol dur et boueux. La neige sale formait une ornière le long du ruisseau. Enfin cette neige devenait la neige sur les marches, les marquises et les façades des petits hôtels. Bourrelets, corniches, paquets lourds de choses légères, au lieu d'épaissir les lignes, faisaient flotter autour une sorte d'émotion, de pressentiment, et grâce à cette neige qui luisait d'elle-même, avec la douceur des montres au radium, l'âme du luxe traversait les pierres, se faisait visible, devenait ce velours qui rapetissait la cité, la meublait, l'enchantait, la transformait en salon fantôme.
>
> (Jean Cocteau, *Les enfants terribles*, Le Livre de Poche, 1976: 11)

> The hard muddy ground had already been smashed, churned up, crushed, stamped into slides by children on their way to school. The soiled snow made ruts along the gutter. But the snow had also become the snow on porches, steps, and house-fronts: featherweight packages, mats, cornices, odds and ends of wadding, ethereal yet crystallized, seemed, instead of blurring the outlines of the stone, to quicken it, to imbue it with a kind of presage.
>
> Gleaming with the soft effulgence of a luminous dial, the snow's incandescence, self-engendered, reached inward to probe the very soul of luxury and draw it forth through stone till it was visible, till it was that fabric magically upholstering the Cité, shrinking it and transforming it into a phantom drawing-room.
>
> (Translation by Rosamund Lehmann, 1955, in
> *Les Enfants Terribles*, Penguin Books, 1961: 9)

The translator took the decision to restructure the first sentence, by **fronting** the repetitive past participles, finishing with the children, probably in order to give greater emphasis to the actions. But Cocteau's description is far from being purely physical: everything is seen through a dual lens: what we see and how it affects us. Words are not just words but impressions too, whether of reality or fantasy.

An interesting topic for discussion is the use of **neologisms** and coined terms in fantasy and children's literature and the challenges they pose. For example, in J. K. Rowling's first Harry Potter book – *Harry Potter and the Philosopher's Stone* – the German and Italian translations follow a different strategy for some proper nouns: *Muggle* (someone not born into a magical family and without magical powers) becomes *Muggel* in German, while in Italian, it is translated *Babbano*. Clearly, German has an advantage over Italian in terms of sound, given the Teutonic matrix of the source and target languages; however, *Babbano* (from *babbeo*, a regional word from central Italy meaning someone a bit simple or gullible) does at least convey the disdain felt by the magic community in the book for Muggles. Interestingly, the term *No-maj* appears to be more popular in the United States than Muggle! Another divergence between the German and Italian versions is the list of Houses at Hogwarts school: the German text retains all four English names (Hufflepuff, Ravenclaw, Gryffindor and Slytherin), while the Italian translates them all (*Tassorosso*: red badger; *Corvonero*: black crow; *Grifondoro*: golden gryphon; *Serpeverde*: green snake). The translated forms do reflect the author's intention to some extent: Hufflepuff's emblem is a badger (though not a red one), a raven is a member of the crow family, but Gryffindor is a golden lion (not a gryphon), while Slytherin is a snake, usually not green but on a green background. Two other invented names in Italian are *Professor McGranitt* (for Professor McGonagall) and *Albus Silente* (Albus Dumbledore). However, in the Spanish translation, all the invented proper nouns are kept in English. In 2015, the *Guardian* published an interesting article by Anna Bradley on translation challenges in the Harry Potter books, which are not only lexical and contextual, but also cultural:

> The wizarding world changes ... when you cast an eye over the Italian translation. Albus Dumbledore inexplicably becomes Albus Silente, despite the fact that almost all the other language versions keep his original name. The French, German and the Finnish are all perfectly content with Dumbledore; not surprisingly, considering it takes its etymological roots from an English dialect word for bumblebee. Dumbledore is a fun word in English, calling to mind a cheerful character, whilst Silente is much sterner. Dumbledore may be quietly pensive at times, but he is far from silent.

Bradley also points out potential pitfalls for those translators brave enough to take on such challenges:

> A good translator then, must not only have a superb grasp of the language itself but also the culture surrounding it. Translation becomes an art and a

knowledgeable translator is paramount. Otherwise, you run the risk of errors in interpretation as well as bad choices, detracting from the quality of the work that caused it to be translated in the first place.

(www.theguardian.com/childrens-books-site/2015/sep/11/
harry-potter-in-translation-albus-silente-dumbledore)

(See Chapter 3 Part 3 for comparisons of Harry Potter translations.)

Moving to a contemporary urban context, translators working in the field of youth culture or young adult novels need to be aware of the emergence of new social dialects, such as Multicultural London English (MLE). An article by Sanjana Varghese in the *New Statesman* on 26 August 2017, "Big Up MLE – The Origins of London's 21st Century Slang," described MLE as a **sociolect** or "multiethnolect" used by urban working-class British young people. This phenomenon is not confined to English: a similar trend has been identified in other countries, such as Germany, where a multilingual hybrid of German and Turkish has evolved (www. hurriyetdailynews.com/german-teens-pick-up-on-turkish-slang-14827, accessed on 18.10.18).

Language change can affect your translation strategy in many ways. For instance, in November 1994, a theatre group from the Düsseldorfer Schauspielhaus performed *Romeo and Juliet* at the London Barbican in a late twentieth-century German translation by Frank Gunther, with Shakespeare's own words displayed as surtitles above the stage. This was a memorable example that highlights the issue of how language changes over time (Shakespeare Survey, Vol 49, 28 Nov. 2002, p. 278, CUP). Many English teachers and students of German in the audience found themselves able to understand the play far better than they had ever done before because the actors were using language that a contemporary German-speaking audience could relate to, making Shakespeare more accessible to modern teenagers.

In 2015, Susan Bassnett addressed the problem of linguistic change in the *ITI Bulletin*, making a rather poignant comment: "Those who can see Shakespeare in their own language are more privileged, it would seem, than those who are doomed to have contact with Shakespeare in the English of 400 years ago." She wondered why there was such strong opposition to translating Shakespeare into modern English, pointing out that many of his jokes were no longer funny because the language had changed since Shakespeare's time ("Neither Rhyme nor Reason," *ITI Bulletin*, September–October 2015: 26–27). The irony is that it was Shakespeare in translation that breathed fresh life into European literature in the eighteenth century! In 2015, *Macbeth* was translated into modern Irish by Seán O Tarpaigh, and a Scottish Gaelic version was performed in Edinburgh in 2014. The fact is that most directors may feel quite comfortable with staging a production in modern dress yet appear to regard a universally comprehensible modern English version as being a step too far.

In her eulogy of the late Czech translator Jiři Josek, Susan Bassnett explains how he had felt his task was to *make Shakespeare function in the here and now.*

He believed that the translator "should be able to read between the lines and relate to the political and ideological atmosphere of the time when the play was produced" ("Good night, sweet prince," *ITI Bulletin*, November–December 2018: 28–29).

To have full control of the lexis (the words or terminology) you use, you need to understand semantic fields. They are words that fall within the same area of meaning. "Boat" is a **superordinate**.

Each of the following words is a **hyponym**. They all describe some very different and specific kinds of boats: canoe, dinghy, dugout, ferry, houseboat, hydrofoil, lifeboat, pedalo. Clearly, if the author refers to a very specific type of vessel, you should be equally specific in your translation, unless, of course, there is a **lexical gap** and there is no direct equivalent in your target language.

If the target language lacks a specific noun, then you could use a noun with an adjective added to make it more specific. Writers use details to give their stories an authentic feel, so it is important to convey the meaning as fully as possible.

Register can create a combined challenge: of interpretation, lexical choice and cultural orientation. For example, a novel set in the Regency period may well contain social registers crafted to appear as authentic period speech, as in this excerpt from Georgette Heyer's *A Civil Contract*, first published by William Heinemann in 1961, where Adam (upper class) is having a conversation with a certain Mr Chawleigh, who is rather lower on the social ladder and "knows his place" in society. Adam comments,

> "Women of consideration don't despise their parents, sir."
> "No, but they don't have to fob 'em off on the ton! said Mr Chawleigh. . . . I take it very kind of you, my lord, but to my way of thinking mushrooms like me aping the Quality don't take: I'd as lief be a Cit as a counter-coxcomb!"
> (Heyer, G. *A Civil Contract*, Pan Books, 1987: 110)

Contemporary critics were dismissive of Heyer's Regency novels, but as Christopher Fowler points out, "The gap between popularity and peer respect was created largely by Heyer's worldwide readers, who lapped up the romances while failing to notice their favourite author's meticulous attention to period detail" (in *The Book of Forgotten Authors*, 2017, Riverrun, London: 155). Despite what Fowler terms "awkward language," he acknowledges that "her late comedies of manners now best stand the test of time and exhibit a nicely cynical wit" (2017: 156).

The translator must decide from the outset what strategy to adopt in transposing any particular social registers the author uses, such as period language or **pastiche**, regional variation or **dialect**, slang or jargon. For example, "quaint" language pastiche may alternate with modern descriptive discourse, creating not only lexical and cultural challenges but also a need for careful **cohesion**.

Pause for thought: How might you approach the translation of a novel that relies in large part on the use of language pastiche to create a historic and/or social impression? If you translate out of English, consider translating the preceding text.

ORGANISATION AND LOGIC

When analysing the source text, you will find it helpful to look at the way the content is structured into sentences and paragraphs, bearing in mind that the syntax may not work as effectively in the target text because grammatical conventions vary from language to language. For instance, in languages such as German and Russian, where the nouns are declined into various cases according to their function, with the Nominative case for the subject, the Accusative case for the object, the Genitive for the possessive and so on, this grammatical feature is often used to achieve cohesion so that one sentence flows smoothly into the next. In German and some Romance languages, it is not unusual to find sentences that begin with a direct or indirect object, so the sentence usually has to be restructured when translated into English.

Syntax is sometimes a problem, for example, in the 2010 translation of *Doctor Zhivago* by Volokhonsky and Pevear, according to Anna Pasternak Slater. She quotes examples of un-English syntax, "*Yura was pleased that he would again meet Nika*" to illustrate how "Sustained, low-level unease is intensified by un-English word-order."

Pause for thought: How would you have restructured this sentence from the 2010 version?

At the turn there would *appear*, and after a moment vanish, *the seven-mile panorama* of Kologrivovo.

The inversion of the subject (*the seven-mile panorama*) and verb (*would appear*) is not natural usage in English, and you may need to change the order of these to make the text flow naturally and reduce the **processing effort** that the reader of the translation has to put in to grasp the meaning.

In her *Translator's Afterword* for the 2006 English version of Orhan Pamuk's *The Black Book*, Maureen Freely describes the *devrik cümle*, a device used by

Turkey's leading writers. It is "a sentence – usually a very long sentence – in which words appear in an order different from that ordained by custom and practice, and cascading clauses create a series of expectations that are subverted by the verb at the very end." She adds, "The poet Murat Nemat-Nejat has described Turkish as a language that can evoke a thought unfolding." The accepted view, especially among bilingual Turks, according to Freely, is that the translator should pay close attention to the sentence's "inner logic," but it's the music of Turkish that she loves, so she prefers to "begin there, with the music." To her, the challenge presented by Turkish prose was to "reorder the various parts of the sentence in a way that allowed it to unfold and reveal its heart." First, she needed to understand how Pamuk's long sentences "contributed to the narrative trance." Any reader of this translation will agree that you are transported into a trance by the cadences she creates (Freely M, Afterword to Orhan Pamuk's *The Black Book*, 2006, London: Faber & Faber).

You might sometimes receive a translation brief that involves the translation of a film transcript. Although this may not require subtitling as such (which is a specialist skill), it is almost essential for you to see the film in order to ensure not only full comprehension of the source text but also an acceptable level of **coherence**, so that you can replicate the correct links between the ideas.

An example of this is shown in the following. It is taken from a speech given in 1967 at the topping out ceremony for the New National Gallery in Berlin, which is now undergoing renovation. The famous architect Mies van der Rohe was explaining that throughout his life, he had always been searching for what architecture was really about. Each of the sentences translated here matched a different screenshot, and timings were helpfully provided in the German transcript of Mathias Schreiber's screenplay for the film made by Georgia van der Rohe, daughter of the architectural maestro.

I am increasingly convinced that architecture's role is to express our civilisation, in its essential parts. Bringing out not our trivial desires, but what really matters to us.

And this is what I see as the real role of architecture. Indeed, it is a long process and everything I have done was about making this clear. Step by step.

So, you can't invent a new architectural style on Monday morning. That is rather naïve.

Architecture was always a really serious matter. Historical eras were named after it.

And that's how it will stay!

(Source: Translation by Ann Pattison, 2017. The German original is reproduced in the Appendix on p. 130)

MEANING

A detailed account of the various types of meaning as described by Newmark was given in *Thinking English Translation* (Cragie and Pattison, 2018: 31–34), so we shall concentrate here on practical examples of texts (mainly from historical contexts) in which the translator struggles to decipher the implicit meaning and make it accessible, usually to an international audience. In a presentation entitled *Néonationalisme et religion en France*, Philippe Portier wrote,

> [L]e monde romain a tourné le dos à l'histoire: il s'est replié dans une intransigeance qui l'entraîne, comme au temps des chrétientés sacrales, à vouloir englober l'ordre politique dans le corps même de l'Église. On ne peut décidément pas, avec un tel associé, demeurer dans la formule partenariale inaugurée par le Premier consul.

The term *le Premier consul* (the first consul) was presumably chosen in order to avoid repetition, which is not considered good style in French. Members of the audience who had been through the French education system would be aware of this title and know to whom it referred, but others would probably not, so the target text had to be made more explicit than the source text to avoid any ambiguity. However, this communicative strategy of interpreting the implicit meaning was not considered appropriate in the case of *sacrales*, where the translator adopted a semantic approach. The other English term considered here was *sacred*, but this alternative was rejected because the author could have used the French *sacrées* but had chosen not to do so. Parallel texts indicated that *sacral* is found in both languages and would be familiar to English-speaking academics. Here is the English version:

> Rome turned its back on history, retreating into an intransigence that filled it with the desire to encompass the political order within the very body of the Church, as it had done in the days of sacral Christianity. It was quite impossible, with such an associate, to stick to the partnership formula established by Napoleon.

The preceding passage illustrates how expansion of the source text may sometimes be necessary in order to make the implicit meaning of cultural references in the source text accessible to the reader of the target text. This is sometimes necessary where the reader of the target text is not likely to have received the same **cognitive inputs** (knowledge absorbed from one's education and life experience within a given culture) as a reader of the source text. Expanding a text is not the same as embellishing it (see *Culture*). The latter strategy involves translator intrusion, that is, the addition of new information content that was not even implied by the author.

When translating or writing descriptive passages that involve the senses, a different kind of meaning defined by David Bellos as "The kind of meaning that things have just by themselves" is key. In *Is That a Fish in Your Ear?* (2013, London: Penguin Books), Bellos refers to this as symptomatic meaning (2013: 67–72). He explains, "Smells, noises, physical sensations, the presence of this or that natural or manufactured object have symptomatic meanings all the time." In his example of someone lost in a forest, the smell of coffee is not merely a pleasant and tantalising aroma but brings this man the reassurance that he is not far from the place where his fellow hikers have pitched camp.

VIEWPOINT

In academic publications, authors will usually adopt an impersonal tone and an objective viewpoint, except perhaps when reporting on their own specific findings, in which case, they are likely to use "we." In fiction, the viewpoint is less clear-cut, and it may be only after a few pages that you can determine whose perspective the story is told from. Some recent bestselling novels tell the tale from an unusual viewpoint or even multiple viewpoints. In Markus Zusak's *The Book Thief*, the viewpoint character is Death, and in Alice Sebold's *The Lovely Bones*, it is the spirit of a murdered teenage girl. Finally, in Michael Malpurgo's children's book *War Horse*, the story is told by Joey the horse. In Paula Hawkins's 2015 psychological thriller *The Girl on the Train*, the main viewpoint character, Rachel, is an alcoholic, so the reader is not sure whether her account of events is reliable. In Antony Doerr's *All the Light We Cannot See*, set in St Malo in World War II, the narrative viewpoint alternates from that of a blind French girl to that of a young German soldier who grew up in an orphanage but has a great talent for repairing radios and locating unauthorised transmitters.

Most modern stories are told either in the first person, the third person or the deep third person (which takes you more directly into the character's head). In *Un homme à histoires*, Patrick Rotman uses a first-person viewpoint, but the story is presented as the memoirs of a journalist who observed a number of historical events first-hand and jotted down snippets of conversation in his notebook, so he could quote them later when he wrote his copy. It therefore appears to be a fairly objective account of events that took place in the late 1950s. The narrator Serge tells us, for example,

> Je connaissais l'antienne du député de la Nièvre. À plusieurs reprises, Mitterrand m'avait confié: "Être président du Conseil à soixante ans, c'est à la portée de n'importe qui. Ce qu'il faut, c'est l'être à quarante ans. Il ne lui restait que deux années."
>
> I knew Mitterrand's favourite mantra well enough. He had confided in me on several occasions: "To be President of the Council of Ministers at sixty is

something that's within everyone's grasp. What you need to do is achieve it at forty.

   He had only two years left."

Memoirs are almost inevitably written in the first person. In *Das Leben ist kein Wunschkonzert* (literally *Life Is Not a Request Programme* but with the English title *Memoirs of a German Soldier*), Martina Pelz published the story of her grandfather Hermann Büttgen's life from his boyhood in Cologne during World War I up to the end of World War II (Pelz, 2009, Norderstedt: Books on Demand GmbH). Because he had left behind a legacy of written records and photographs, she decided to retain his use of the first person. After discussion with the client, the translators added an English synopsis in the third person, giving a brief overview of Hermann's life. This replaced Hermann's own preface, written in the first person on a rather personal note, asking one of his descendants to complete his initial attempt at researching the family history. The translators (a team consisting of three MA graduates from the University of Westminster led by Ann Pattison) also kept to the first-person viewpoint. After all, the translation had been commissioned on behalf of Hermann's English-speaking relatives and descendants, and it was felt important to maintain the personal touch.

> **Pause for thought**: Can you think of any instances where the translator would feel it necessary to change the viewpoint or narrative perspective? When might "translator intrusion" of this kind be justifiable?

STYLISTIC FEATURES

The literary translator also needs to consider a number of style-related factors, not all of which are immediately obvious unless the author has a particularly marked style or **idiolect** or has adopted an unconventional technique. Modern writers may try to stand out in this way or decide that a different approach is what the story dictates. In *Golden Hill*, for instance, Francis Spufford decided to tell his tale in the archaic manner and style of an eighteenth-century novel. The book's opening sentence is seventeen lines long, although the general trend at the time of its publication in 2017 was "the shorter the better." Because this was such a deliberate and marked literary device, anyone planning to translate *Golden Hill* into another language would need to replicate this somehow without alienating the reader. Spufford uses the archaic word *brig* instead of *ship* or *vessel* and formal expressions such as "he meaning by the offer to signal his esteem." In the German version by Jan Schönherr, entitled *Neu York* (Rowohlt: 2017), the translator likewise uses the old-fashioned term *die Brigg* and preserves the syntactic structure in an equally long German sentence.

Another question you might need to consider is *What does the text sound like?*

In the literary field, you need in particular to be aware of the linguistic devices and figures of speech that writers use and then select a strategy or strategies for dealing with them.

Some of the most common figures of speech are alliteration and assonance. **Alliteration** refers to the selection (often deliberate) of words that begin with the same consonant, whereas the use of echoing vowel sounds is known as **assonance**).

Here are a few examples of alliteration from popular cinema and books:

Film titles include *The Fast and the Furious* (2013), *Gone Girl* (2014), *Guardians of the Galaxy* (2014), and *The Wolf of Wall Street* (2013). Alliterative book titles include Ali Smith's *How to Be Both* (2014), F. Scott Fitzgerald's 1925 novel *The Great Gatsby*, and David Walliams' *Grandpa's Great Escape* (2015) and *Gangsta Granny* (2013).

Film titles that feature assonance are *Unfinished Business* (2015), *Safe Haven* (2013) and *Nowhere Boy* (the title of a 2009 film about John Lennon in which the "o" sounds create a haunting effect). This resonates with the Beatles' song "Nowhere Man" (first lines = "He's a real nowhere man, Sitting in his nowhere land, Making all his nowhere plans for nobody." It is the repetition here, as well as the assonance, that makes the song memorable and haunting).

The secret to successfully incorporating such stylistic devices in translation is knowing what words will sound like when they are read aloud. Even if there is no audience involved, the sound of words is important, that is, not just on their own but in combination. Of course, it may not be possible to replicate alliteration or assonance or a metaphor in the equivalent TL words, but this could be done later in the same sentence or paragraph to sustain the mood that the SL author created.

Metaphors, too, can help to convey the mood of a time, place or character. In *The Trouble with Goats and Sheep* (published in 2016 by The Borough Press), a gentle critique of small-town mentalities in an English street during the 1976 heatwave, Joanna Cannon creates some very well-chosen metaphors to convey the mood and mindset of the time. For instance, ten-year-old Grace describes how her friend Tilly "stamped her frown out into the doormat" (2016: 232).

An example of how a translator might handle metaphor can be found in the translation (by Ann Pattison) of *Two Heads of Hussein*, an article by Pierre-Jean Luizard, where the final half-sentence of the ST reads,

la tragédie de Karbala disparaît derrière les lampions et les feux d'artifice.

A literal English translation ("disappears behind the lights and fireworks") would have reduced the impact of the source text, making the article end on a rather flat note, so the translator took the liberty of expanding the sentence and adding a metaphor:

the tragedy of Karbala is drowned in a sea of lights and fireworks.

She considered this solution to be justifiable in order to sustain the author's earlier description of *une veritable marée humaine que les ruelles étroites ne permettent pas d'écouler* (a veritable tide of people that is unable to flow through the narrow lanes). There is also an example of assonance here in the author's use of *ruelles étroites ne permettent pas d'écouler.*

It is not just the sound of words and phrases that you need to think about but the rhythm and cadences of the sentence as a whole. This can affect the choices to be made. You have to decide whether a short conjunction such as "but" would fit in better than one with three or four syllables, such as "however" or "nevertheless."

Some words the writer uses may contain hidden allusions to current cultural trends or icons or even puns. This extract from an article entitled "Tory Masses Hail Boris as He Swoops into Town" by the late Simon Hoggart, which appeared in the *Guardian* on 9 October 2012, illustrates how well-chosen words, images and figures of speech can create a very amusing picture.

He leapt into action, or at least into Euston. Not since Lenin headed towards the Finland station has there been such alarm and terror among the ruling classes.

The humour is achieved by the use of a figure of speech known as **zeugma** when the verb *leapt* is used in two different contexts. This is enhanced by the assonance between "action" and "Euston." In addition, there is a political allusion (or reference) to Lenin and the Finland station (where he got off the train on 3 April 1917 to take charge of the Russian Revolution).

Whether you are translating a creative journalistic piece, a fantasy, historical fiction, poetry, or a social science paper that assumes an in-depth knowledge of a particular culture, what you need to develop is a sense of how the writer manipulates language to match the time and context. Only then will you be able to determine the best strategy to reconstruct the source text in your target language.

Analysing, translating, comparing, editing

INTRODUCTION

In Chapter 2, we discussed the analytical criteria that we propose section by section and created a platform for exploration and development of these themes and for activities, through the "Pause for thought" tasks. We also included examples of texts and translations, to give you an idea of the range of aspects and challenges involved in translating literary and semi-literary texts.

The analytical model, set out here in a full version (standard) and a summarised form (fast-track), is designed to help you extract information on the subject, language and culture of the text, so that you gain a holistic view of the nature of the source text and its textual challenges. The analytical model will enable you to prepare a text for translation, as well as consider translation as product.

Chapter 3 has a specifically practical focus and is divided into four parts:

- analysis of four English texts (*Part 1*);
- annotated translations of four English texts into French, German, Italian and Spanish (*Part 2i*); annotated translations of four texts (from French, German, Italian and Spanish) into English (*Part 2ii*);
- translation comparisons (*Part 3*);
- editing translations (*Part 4*).

The analyses we provide in this chapter show how our criteria can be applied, while highlighting the benefits that derive from close reading of the text – an activity that helps you decide how to approach your task and its features. The annotated translations from and into English show how the translators approached their tasks (**macro strategy**) and comment on some of their choices (**micro strategies**). The target text comparisons examine the approaches and solutions adopted in translation of a text, whether in one or two target versions of the same text, while the final part of this chapter looks at editing translated texts.

In the standard version of the analytical model, you will see that each of the *Criteria* is broken down into an *Area* (the themes to be examined), *Features* (specific details) and *Questions*, which invite you to focus on specific issues and perspectives in the source text. The analytical process starts with general information and then explores relevant textual features to establish the role they play in the text. The model has been developed for use in both textual analysis and translation evaluation.

The annotations which accompany the translations in Part 2 identify specific translation challenges and explain how these challenges are approached and resolved by the translator.

STANDARD ANALYTICAL MODEL

Criteria	Area	Features	Questions
Preliminary information	Author	[Name]	Are you familiar with the author?
	Title of work	[Name]	Are you familiar with the source text?
	Theme	Summary of plot/ ideas	What is the main theme of the work?
			Are there various strands/sub-plots in the work?
	Form	Physical form/ layout	What form does the work take?
	Genre	Type of text	Is the text typical of the genre?
	Purpose	Of text/of translation	Whom is the text for? Who are the end users? Is there a translation brief?
Time	Date of first edition/ publication	[Date]	Which edition (where applicable) of the work is the text taken from?
	Date/s of translation/s	[Date/s]	Which version of the translation is it?
			Do any translations contain an introduction or translator's notes?
	Timeframes in the work/text	Techniques used for expressing time in the work	How does the action progress? (forwards, backwards, circular, flashbacks, combination, and so on)
	Other timeframes	Time of writing, reading, translation, publishing, and so on	How do these timeframes affect the reading/translation process?

(*Continued*)

(Continued)

Criteria	Area	Features	Questions
Context	Setting	Logistical Linguistic	Where do the actions take place? How are the semantic and lexical units inserted in the surrounding discourse?
Culture	Cultural features in source text (*text analysis*)	Proper nouns, exoticisms, quotations, third language references, and so on	Which cultural features are of particular significance, and why?
	Cultural features in target text (*translation analysis*)	Proper nouns, exoticisms, quotations, third language references, and so on	Are cultural references adequately and appropriately transferred into the target text? Is there any **localisation**?
	"Cultural share" of stakeholders	Cultural environment of author, reader, translator, and so on	What do the various beliefs, values and experiences of the stakeholders bring to the work?
Language	Source **language structure** (*text analysis*)	Grammar/syntax	How complex is the structure of sentences, syntax and grammar in the source language? Are there any unusual or significant features?
	Target language structure (*translation analysis*)	Grammar/syntax	How complex is the structure of sentences, syntax and grammar in the target language? What similarities/differences exist between the source/ target language structures?
	Source language lexis and register (*text analysis*)	Lexis; social level of language (register)	Is the source language standard, or does it diverge from standard lexis/ registers?
	Target language lexis and register (*translation analysis*)	Lexis; social level of language (register)	Is the target language use of lexis and register in line with the source, or are there notable differences?

Criteria	Area	Features	Questions
	Source language organisation and logic (*text analysis*)	Sentences/ paragraphing; cohesion and coherence	How is the discourse organised in the source text? How cohesive and coherent is it?
	Target language organisation and logic (*translation analysis*)	Sentences/ paragraphing; cohesion and coherence	Does organisation differ in the target language? Is this due to differences between the languages or translator intervention? How cohesive and coherent is it?
Meaning	Clarity and comprehension of source text (*text analysis*)	Sense of source language discourse; meaning of semantic units and whole text	Is the meaning of the source text always clear, or does it need interpretation?
	Clarity and comprehension of target text (*translation analysis*)	Sense of target language discourse; meaning of semantic units and whole text	Is there any difference in nuance or interpretation/ meaning between source/ target languages?
Viewpoint	Viewpoint	Author's voice; relationship with readers; reader reception	Are there multiple viewpoints or perspectives in the source? If so, how are these reflected and conveyed in the target?
	Source/target language bias (language)	Semantic/ communicative	Does the translation follow the source language closely, or does it communicate more directly with the readers?
	Source/target language bias (culture)	Foreignization/ domestication	Does the translation maintain a source culture bias or attempt to naturalise cultural items in the target?
Style	Source language stylistic features (*text analysis*)	Author's idiolect; figurative language; punctuation; paragraphing, and so on	What particular stylistic features are typical of the author's work? How important are they for transfer to the target?

(*Continued*)

(Continued)

Criteria	Area	Features	Questions
	Target language stylistic features (*translation analysis*)	Author's idiolect; figurative language; punctuation; paragraphing; and so on	How effectively have stylistic features and author idiosyncrasies been transferred to the target?
Translation challenges	Identifying the main challenges under the criteria listed above.		

FAST-TRACK ANALYTICAL MODEL

Preliminaries	Work, author, date, theme, type of text, purpose/brief of translation
Timeframes	Timeframes in work; time of writing; time of reading; time of translation
Context	Setting: Where? What?/Discourse
Culture	Cultural features in source/target; "cultural share" of stakeholders
Language	Structure (grammar, syntax); lexis/register; cohesion/coherence
Meaning	Clarity and comprehension of source/target text
Viewpoint	Viewpoints expressed in work; reflects source/target culture bias
Style	Author's style of writing/expression; use of figurative language
Challenges	Most conspicuous translation challenges

PART 1: ANALYSES OF ENGLISH TEXTS

The four texts used in this part have been chosen to reflect different literary genres: early twentieth-century fiction, recent fiction, humour/literature and academic writing. Other extracts from the same sources are used for the translations out of English in Part 2, for the purpose of continuity.

Text 1: Early twentieth-century fiction

He trailed his umbrella behind him over the grass-grown paths; staying here and there to read some time-worn inscription; stooping a little broodingly over the dark green graves. Not for the first time during the long laborious convalescence that had followed apparently so slight an indisposition, a fleeting sense almost as if of an intelligible remorse had overtaken him, a vague thought that behind all these past years, hidden as it were from his daily life, lay something not yet quite reckoned with. How often as a boy had he been rapped into a galvanic activity out of the deep reveries he used to fall into – those fits of a kind of fishlike day-dream. How often, and even far beyond boyhood, had he found himself bent on some distant thought or fleeting vision that the sudden clash of self-possession had made to seem quite illusory, and yet had left so strangely haunting. And now the old habit had stirred out of its long sleep, and, through the gate that Influenza in departing had left ajar, had returned upon him.

Preliminary information: From *The Return*, a novel by Walter De La Mare (first published in 1922); this excerpt comes from the edition published in 1936 by Penguin Books. The passage is from the beginning of the book (pp. 9–10): Arthur Lawford is convalescing after an illness and wanders into a graveyard. (De La Mare is better known as a poet. This may have relevance in the analysis, given the poetic nature of some of the language here.)

Time: The here and now, reminiscences and recurrent thoughts. This use of time would be familiar to the reader/translator, despite the fact that the book is almost a hundred years old.

Context: *Setting:* a graveyard somewhere in England in the 1920s. *Linguistic context:* From the beginning of the book (a long initial paragraph), describing Lawford's slow convalescence and his melancholy state of mind.

Culture: References to a graveyard, boyhood, day-dreams, melancholy. All universal concepts that the reader/translator can identify with.

Language: The structure is quite complex in terms of sentence structure, with phrase after phrase imitating the thoughts, recollections and realisations going through Lawford's mind.

Lexis: Some unusual words and phrases (*rapped into a galvanic activity*; *sudden clash of self-possession*).

Cohesion and coherence: The text is cohesive and coherent, but the "stream of consciousness" style would need careful treatment in translation.

Meaning: The meaning of some descriptions of his reveries and emotions needs to be teased out and clarified: for example, what exactly is meant by a "fishlike day-dream"? Interpretation is needed in order to recreate concepts and impressions accurately and appropriately.

Viewpoint: The viewpoint is third person, through the eyes of Lawford. It is subjective. Even objective elements (umbrella, convalescence, and so on) take on a melancholy perspective.

Stylistic features: Poetic feel to the language; use of simile and metaphor, alliteration and assonance (green graves, fits/fishlike, day-dream, long laborious, stooping/broodingly).

Translation challenges: Balancing the standard and poetic use of language; avoiding over- and under-translation.

Text 2: Recent fiction

From my cramped vantage point in the back I have a good view of my family's ears. My father's, which stick out from under the brim of the old felt hat he wears to keep twigs and tree sap and caterpillars out of his hair, are large and soft-looking, with long lobes; they're like the ears of gnomes, or those of flesh-coloured, dog-like minor characters in Mickey Mouse comic books. My mother wears her hair pinned back at the sides with bobby-pins, so her ears are visible from the back. They're narrow, with fragile upper edges, like the handles of china cups. My brother's ears are round, like dried apricots, or like the ears of the green-tinged oval-headed aliens from outer space he draws with his coloured pencils. Around and over his ears and down the back of his neck his hair, dark blond and straight, grows in thick wisps. He resists haircuts.

Preliminary information: From *Cat's Eye* by Margaret Atwood (1990) – (II *Silver Paper*, section 4, p. 21). Elaine Risley, a painter, returns to Toronto to find herself overwhelmed by her past. In this excerpt, she reminisces about travelling through Canada by car with her parents and brother as a child.

Time: Written in 1988, timeframe 1940/50s. Childhood memories.

Context: *Setting:* In a car travelling around Canada, like nomads; *Linguistic context:* A single paragraph; layered impressions using short and longer sentences with intermediate punctuation.

Culture: Mid-twentieth century Canada; family life; Mickey Mouse and comic books; aliens; nature (trees, caterpillars, and so on).

Language: Standard, everyday language. Lexis: Descriptive, visual, evocative of childhood, yet language un-childlike. Use of hyphenated word forms. Cohesion and coherence: Cohesive and coherent.

Meaning: The meaning is clear throughout.

Viewpoint: The action and description is all seen through the girl's/narrator's eyes and through her (limited) experience of life, hence the curious similes (dog-like minor characters in Mickey Mouse; ears like dried apricots).

Stylistic features: Graphic description; sequenced impressions; use of similes/ analogy.

Translation challenges: Capturing the child's impressions, which are expressed through language and sentiment. Can the translator identify exactly with the writer's experience? Some specific cultural references may be opaque to speakers of non-western languages.

Text 3: Humour/literature

Why are good authors forgotten?
    Absence doesn't make the heart grow fonder. It makes people think you're dead.

Come along to an author's event some time and listen to the comments we get. Readers will say things like, "I read one of your books when I was twelve," or "I had no idea you were still going. You don't need the money now, surely?" or "My grandmother was a fan of yours, but then she'd read anything, not being able to get out."

It doesn't stop there. One day you find a complete set of your books in a charity shop, suggestive of a house clearance after a death. You perform at a library on a rainy night when the audience is mainly interested in the radiator. Your publisher can never wait to get off the line. Your pants are older than your publicist. Finally you depart the world in penury, and *then* they publish your backlist to great acclaim.

Some years ago I attended a paperback fair in the basement of a dank Victorian hotel that reeked of stale breakfasts and dead salesmen, and found myself the only punter in a room of a hundred haunted-looking booksellers. It felt as if I was attending the wake of an unloved relative. As I loaded my arms with musty pocketbooks I wondered if popular writing was finally redundant. Last year I returned to the same hotel and had to queue for an hour to get in. The fair was mobbed. Then I thought, Vinyl came back, maybe paperbacks are analogue nostalgia.

Preliminary information: From *The Book of Forgotten Authors* by Christopher Fowler. From the introduction to the book (pp. 1–2), which contains short profiles of ninety-nine "forgotten authors."

Time: Published in 2017. Reminiscences as a way of introducing the book.

Context: From the beginning of the introduction, so *tabula rasa*, in which the author "sets out his stall."

Culture: Publishing; personal experiences; booksellers and book fairs; Victorian hotel; charity shop.

Language: Contemporary informal language. Lexis: Standard language, with some pseudo direct speech; present tense and use of "you/your" to make reader live the experiences; Cohesion and coherence: "Scenes" are cohesive, but the overall effect is of a pattern or sequence of classic experiences.

Meaning: The meaning is clear.

Viewpoint: The author describes typical situations, which he wants the reader to imagine experiencing.

Stylistic features: Humour, irony and sarcasm are the leitmotiv and *raison d'être* of this passage.

Translation challenges: Finding ways to capture and transfer the irony through the use of informal language, without making the translation sound curious, awkward or overly colloquial. Conveying the images/impressions graphically, as the author does.

Text 4: Academic text

It was not until he turned forty-three that he managed to secure gallery representation. Dubuffet referred to the twenty-something years after leaving the Académie as his "prehistory," and while he destroyed most of his early works, a handful of paintings do remain. Scrutinizing these pre-1940s tableaus, art historian Aruna D'Souza categorizes this period as "Picasso-esque," composed mostly of artworks belonging to a "classical-Cubist mode." Perhaps it was because his work seemed derivative of what was already on the market that Dubuffet failed to actualize his career until he was middle-aged. To differentiate his art from the rest, he would need to look beyond the Parisian art bubble – a precedent set by a number of avant-garde artists. Drawing parallels between Dubuffet's search and similar quests for non-Western inspiration, outsider art expert Lucienne Peiry noted:

Artists felt a need to free themselves from their tradition and were searching for new values and landmarks, resulting in a kaleidoscopic quest for otherness: Delacroix left for the East in search of love with the splendor of the South Seas, Picasso was fascinated by strange tribal works, and Kandinsky marveled at the engravings of folk artists.

Perhaps originality seemed more accessible away from home, beyond the cultural forces of familiar surroundings. . . . So-called primitive people were thought to possess a "spontaneity" that Western civilization was believed to have lost. Favoured non-Western cultures of the avant-garde were typically non-industrial and were therefore interpreted as being somehow closer to nature.

Preliminary information: From *Platform*, Vol. 11, "Authenticity," Autumn 2017 – *Jean Dubuffet & Art Brut: The Creation of an Avant-Garde Identity* by Antonia Dapena-Tretter.

Time: Published in 2017. Partly biographical. Focuses on specific moments in Dubuffet's artistic career. Contemporary perspective in art historians' comments and author's narrative.

Context: From near the beginning of the article.

Culture: Multiple cultural references: art history and art historians/critics; Académie; gallery; prehistory; engravings; folk artists; tableaus; Dubuffet's life and works; outsider art; art experts Aruna D'Souza and Lucienne Peiry; Picasso-esque, classical-Cubist; Delacroix, Kandinsky; the East; Parisian art bubble; avant-garde; South Seas; Western civilisation; non-Western cultures; tribal/primitive.

Language: American English (splendor; marveled); high academic register, assuming an informed audience (e.g., otherness, derivative, actualize); quotes; figurative language (kaleidoscopic quest).

Meaning: The text needs careful reading in order to understand a) the cultural references and b) the author's (and quoted expert's) style and register.

Viewpoint: Three perspectives: author/narrator; D'Souza; Peiry.

Stylistic features: See *Language*.

Translation challenges: Comprehension; familiarity with specialist subject matter (research may be needed); ability to achieve an appropriate style and register whilst conveying the information or opinion accurately.

> **Pause for thought**: For practice, choose either analysis 1 or 2, and produce it in a fast-track version. If you translate from English, imagine you have been asked by a publisher to translate into your target language the whole book from which your extract is taken and to give your answer with some urgency. How would you go about responding to the request, and what factors would you need to take into consideration before responding?

PART 2: ANNOTATED TRANSLATIONS

2i: Texts from English into German, Spanish, French and Italian

The following texts are taken from the same sources as the ones analysed in the preceding section. The aim is to show how textual analysis helps to pave the way for translation, via text exploration to direct contact, interaction and decision-making. Each translation is accompanied by a macro strategy and a set of six micro strategies with comments.

Source text 1 – English into German

From *The Return* by Walter De La Mare (1936: 22).

"He was utterly wearied, but he walked on for a long while with a dogged unglancing[1] pertinacity and without looking behind him. Then he rested under the dew-sodden hedgeside and buried his face in his hands.

Once, indeed, he did turn and grind[2] his way back with hard uplifted face for many minutes, but at the meeting with an old woman who in the late dusk passed him unheeded[3] on the road, he stopped again, and after standing awhile looking down upon the dust, trying to gather up the tangled threads of his thoughts, he once more set off homewards.

Vollkommen ermattet setzte er seinen Weg eine Weile fort, mit verbissener Beharrlichkeit, unbeirrt[1] und ohne zurückzublicken. An einer tauschweren Hecke am Straßenrand hielt er Rast und vergrub das Gesicht in den Händen.

Schließlich machte er doch einmal kehrt und schleppte sich[2] mit starr erhobenem Gesicht eine Zeit lang zurück; erst bei der Begegnung mit einer alten Frau, die er in der späten Dämmerung im Vorbeigehen kaum wahrnahm[3], hielt er wieder inne und senkte den Blick auf den Straßenstaub, in dem Versuch seine wirren Gedanken zu fassen, um dann schließlich einmal mehr den Weg heimwärts einzuschlagen.

(Continued)

(Continued)

It was clear, starry, and quite dark[4] when he reached the house. The lamp at the roadside obscurely lit its breadth and height.[5] Lamp-light within, too, was showing yellow between the Venetian blinds; a cold gas-jet[5] gleamed out of the basement window.	*In sternenklarer Dunkelheit[4] erreichte er das Haus, das sich im fahlen Licht der Straßenlampe befremdlich groß[5] abzeichnete. Von innen fiel gelbes Lampenlicht durch die Holzjalousien; der kalte Strahl einer Gaslampe[5] schien durch das Fenster im Untergeschoß.*
He seemed bereft now of all desire or emotion, simply the passive witness of things external in a calm which, though he scarcely realised its cause, was an exquisite solace and relief.	*Er empfand jetzt keinerlei Gefühle oder Wünsche, war lediglich ein passiver Betrachter äußerer Dinge und vernahm eine innere Ruhe, deren Ursache ihm zwar nicht klar war, die aber wohltuenden Trost und Erleichterung brachte.*
His senses were intensely sharpened with sleeplessness. The faintest sound belled[6] clear and keen on his ear. The thinnest beam of light besprinkled[6] his eyes with curious brilliance."	*Seine Sinne waren von der Schlaflosigkeit aufs Höchste geschärft. Der leiseste Ton schlug glockenklar[6] an sein Ohr; der feinste Lichtstrahl benetzte[6] seine Augen mit seltsamer Brillanz.*

BRIEF

The passage is to be translated as a sample for a publisher who is looking for a suitable translator for the whole book. The setting (location, characters and period) is to be retained in the translation, an English mystery novel with a strong psychological dimension. Language, register and tone should chime with the contemporary reader.

MACRO STRATEGY

In light of the brief, particular attention was paid to the artistic and aesthetic qualities of the piece and the sustained creation of mood. Lexical choices, style and tone should maintain literary flair and expressivity, recreate the surreal atmosphere of a transcendent reality and appeal on an auditory level through sound and rhythm. Any "period feeling" or datedness now perceived in the language of the original was not intended at the time of writing (1910) and was therefore avoided in the TT. The new reader should experience the character's personal trauma, his (imagined?) possession, transformation and alienation, without being hampered by antiquated language.

MICRO STRATEGIES AND COMMENTS

[1] *Recasting*: The noun phrase "dogged unglancing pertinacity," which has a wonderfully poetic rhythm, needed recasting in the TL, to avoid semantic reiteration

and loss of flow through separating commas between adjectives. In a syntactic shift, *unbeirrt*, now used as an adverb, connects with the verb phrase *er setzte . . . Weg fort* where it retains the intended emphasis.

[2] *Lexis*: The verb "to grind" in the sense of "to walk" is unusual, possibly chosen for its auditory effect, and alludes to the character's inner resistance or reluctance to walk back. An amplification on the lines of *er ging schweren Schrittes* was initially considered, as the genitive form would also serve to enhance the literary quality. But in the co-text of the other qualifying phrase, "with hard uplifted face," a simpler verb (*sich schleppen*) was preferred.

[3] **Ambiguity**: The unusual and dated qualifier "unheeded" (full meaning "noticed but disregarded") at first seemed structurally ambiguous: (a) Did the woman pass by without being heeded by him, or (b) was he unheeded by the woman who passed him? In the narrow context of the passage both readings seem plausible: (a) because he was exhausted and (b) because his appearance had changed. However, stylistic and syntactical examination indicates that *the woman* is the likely referent of the past participle *unheeded*, so the first of the two interpretations was adopted in the translation. To maintain coherence in this very long sentence, the perspective was changed in the relative clause, so that *he* is the subject of the action throughout.

[4] *Emphasis*: The sequence of three adjectives "Clear, starry and quite dark" is an example of the "rule of three," used to maximise rhetorical impact and reinforce the point in time (i.e., "by night"). This technique is equally established in the TL; however, to avoid a stylistically weak beginning, "*Es war*," some recasting was necessary. Compounding two adjectives into one and nominalising the third improved economy and flow, whilst retaining all semantic elements to contextualise the passing of time and changed scenery.

[5] *Expansion*: Contextual information was added to clarify the somewhat intangible reference "breadth and height." A search for "house" throughout the whole novel revealed a more meaningful occurrence: "Lawford looked across in his mind at his square ungainly house. . . . He tried to repress a shudder" (Chapter 18). This insight was used to improve coherence and help the TL reader of the TL passage to see with the character's eyes. Another example where specific meaning was added is the expansion of the cultural reference "gas-jet" to *Strahl einer Gaslampe* to enable the reader to visualise the scene.

[6] *Imagery*: The last two sentences illustrate De la Mare's concern for the sound that written words carry. The unconventional use of "bell" as a verb, in a phrase further distinguished by alliteration, assonance and rhyme, is highly poetic. The adjective *glockenklar* was chosen for its velar and alveolar consonants to recreate the sound effect. Another example of poetic licence is the verb "besprinkle," often associated with a liquid and here possibly used to carry forward the audible dimension. The translation sought to capture the imagery with the verb *benetzen* (*berühren* would have been a less marked and safer choice but was rejected for that reason).

Source text 2 – English into Spanish

From *Cat's Eye* by Margaret Atwood (1990: 206).

"The school[1] we go to is called Burnham High School. It's recently built, oblong in shape,[2] flat-roofed, undecorated, unrevealing,[3] sort of like a factory. It's the latest thing in modern architecture. Inside, it has long corridors with mottled floors of something that looks like granite but is not. The yellowish walls are lined with dark-green lockers, and there's an auditorium and a P.A. system.

Every morning we have announcements over the P.A. system. First we have a Bible reading and prayers. I bow my head during the prayers but I refuse to pray, though I don't know why I do this. After the prayers the Principal tells us of coming events, and he also warns us to pick up our chewing-gum wrappers and not to moon around in the halls like old married couples.

His name is Mr. MacLeod, although everyone calls him Chrome Dome[4] behind his back because he's bald on top[5]; and he's a Scot by affiliation. Burnham High has a school plaid, a school crest with a thistle and a couple of those Scottish knives they stick in their socks, and a Gaelic motto. The plaid, the crest, the motto, and the school colours all belong to Mr. MacLeod's personal clan.

In the front hall, alongside the Queen, hangs a portrait of Dame Flora MacLeod with her two bagpipe-playing grandsons posed outside Dunvegan Castle. We are encouraged to think of this castle as our ancestral castle, and of Dame Flora as our spiritual leader."

El instituto[1] al que vamos se llama Burnham High School. Se construyó recientemente, tiene forma alargada[2], tejado plano, y apenas tiene decoración ni nada especial[3]. Se parece a una fábrica. Es lo último en arquitectura moderna. En su interior hay largos pasillos con manchas en el suelo de algo que parece granito, pero no lo es. En las paredes amarillentas se alinean taquillas de color verde oscuro, y hay un salón de actos y un sistema de megafonía.

Todas las mañanas se hacen anuncios por megafonía. Primero una lectura de la Biblia y oraciones. Inclino la cabeza durante las oraciones, pero me niego a rezar, aunque no sé por qué lo hago. Después de las oraciones, el director anuncia los próximos eventos y también nos recuerda que recojamos los envoltorios de chicle y no deambulemos por los pasillos como los matrimonios mayores.

Se llama Don MacLeod, aunque todos lo llaman "bola de billar"[4] a sus espaldas porque es calvo,[5] y es escocés de afiliación. Burnham High School tiene un tartán, un emblema del colegio con un cardo y un par de esos cuchillos escoceses que se incrustan en los calcetines, y un lema gaélico. El tartán, el emblema, el lema y los colores del colegio pertenecen al clan personal de Don MacLeod.

En la entrada, junto a la reina, hay un retrato de Dame Flora MacLeod con sus dos nietos tocando la gaita, posando delante del Castillo Dunvegan. Nos animan a concebir este castillo como nuestro castillo ancestral, y a Dame Flora como nuestra líder espiritual."

BRIEF

The passage is to be translated as a test for a publisher seeking literary translators into Spanish.

MACRO STRATEGY

The source text is a passage from recent fiction – a narrative and descriptive piece with a recurrent use of adjectives. In the first paragraph, it is important to preserve the graphic description of Burnham High School, which is possible given the richness of Spanish vocabulary in terms of nouns, adjectives and adverbs (see comments 2 and 3). Since the action and description is seen through the main character's eyes and experience, an effort has been made to preserve the tone of the narration and stylistic features using similar figurative language (i.e., similes, metaphors, analogies and images) to recreate the same setting and scene for the target readership. This strategy has been used to select, for example, a suitable nickname for the principal in Spanish that still conveys the same expressive meaning as the original term (see comment 4). The use of transposition has also been prioritised to produce a cohesive and coherent piece of work that fully complies with stylistic expectations for literary and semi-literary texts in Spanish (see comment 2).

MICRO STRATEGIES AND COMMENTS

[1] *Cultural item*: Education systems differ considerably across countries, as does the terminology used to refer to different stages of education. For example, the terms *colegio* and *escuela* are often used indiscriminately in many countries in Spanish America, while the term *colegio* is more widely used in Spain to refer to primary education. However, the term *instituto* is used exclusively for secondary education. The context provided in subsequent passages of the book, including references to the age of the boys in the school ("Some are fifteen, almost sixteen") justify the use of the term *instituto* in this context.

[2] *Lexis*: **Literal translation** rarely works between languages. For instance, the expression "oblong in shape" literally transferred as *alargada en forma* would produce a stylistically awkward rendering in Spanish. This problem can be solved with a transposition; in other words, by replacing the prepositional phrase "in shape" with syntax consisting of a verb (to have) followed by a noun (shape) and adjective (oblong) [i.e. *tiene forma alargada*].

[3]*Lexis*: The widely used prefix "un" in English sometimes has a direct equivalent in Spanish, for instance *des-* (e.g., *deshacer*) or *in-* [i- before l or r] (e.g., *irreal*). However, such cases are unusual, and the translator often needs to resort to the use of indefinite adverbs such as *poco* or *nada* followed by the corresponding noun,

or adverbs suggesting the opposite meaning (e.g., *apenas*; *no*) followed by a verbal phrase. The terms "undecorated" and "unrevealing" do not have a straightforward equivalent in Spanish, but the same meaning can still be conveyed by using the adverbs *apenas* and *nada* and paraphrasing the meaning (i.e., unrevealing – not very special).

[4] *Proper noun*: There are several translation procedures for translating figurative language, such as metaphors, including reproducing the same metaphor and image in the target language, replacing the image and metaphor in the target language or transforming the metaphor to sense. For instance, the adjective *pelón* ("baldie"; "hairless") and *bola de billar* (**literal meaning**: *billiard ball*) could be considered equivalents of the expression "Chrome Dome." Finding a similar image in the target language is the preferred translation strategy to render the same expressive image. Therefore, "Chrome Dome" is translated as *bola de billar*.

[5] **Redundancy**: Omission is a strategy when it is considered unnecessary or inappropriate to reproduce the meaning of a particular expression or signifier. An omission is needed in Spanish to convey the expression "bald on top." The adjective *calvo/a* specifically refers to a person with little or no hair on his or her head. Given that the meaning conveyed by the expression "on top" is already implicit in the term *calvo*, an omission is deemed appropriate in this case. Similarly, at the end of the previous paragraph, if we split up the term *matrimonio* into its sense components, both the notion of relationship and couple are implicit. Therefore, it is not necessary to replicate the idea conveyed by the term "couple."

Source text 3 – English into French

From *The Book of Forgotten Authors* by Christopher Fowler (2017: 72).

Emma Orczy	Emma Orczy
"The Hungarian-born[1] British novelist Baroness Emma Magdolna Rozália Mária Jozefa Borbála 'Emmuska' Orczy de Orci is not unknown but certainly unread in the UK nowadays. Her family left Budapest in fear of a peasant revolution and she fetched up[2] in Great Portland Street, virtually penniless[4]; there weren't too many occupations for a deposed baroness in late nineteenth-century London.[3]	*La baronne Emma Magdolna Rozália Mária Jozefa Borbála "Emmuska" Orczy de Orci, dite Emma Orczy, romancière britannique d'origine hongroise[1] ne nous est pas inconnue, mais elle n'est certes guère lue de nos jours en Grande-Bretagne. Craignant une révolte paysanne, sa famille avait quitté Budapest et elle se retrouva[2] à Londres[3], à Great Portland Street, pratiquement sans un sou ; dans la capitale britannique[3] à la fin du dix-neuvième siècle,[4] perspectives de carrière étaient maigres pour une baronne destituée.*

Emma Orczy	Emma Orczy
Her[5] first novel, *The Emperor's Candlestick*, published in 1899, was a failure, but she started producing pulpish mystery fiction, creating the first female detective with official status, the spirited feminist Lady Molly of Scotland Yard,[6] a logic-minded armchair sleuth. . . . Orczy also had some paintings hung in the Royal Academy.[6]	*En 1899, Emma Orczy[5] publie son premier roman,* Les chandeliers de l'Empereur, *qui n'obtient aucun succès. Elle écrira cependant des romans policiers populaires et créera la première femme détective reconnue officiellement comme telle, la courageuse féministe Lady Molly de Scotland Yard,[6] enquêtrice en fauteuil férue de logique. . . . La baronne Orczy est également l'auteure de tableaux qui sont exposés à la Royal Academy[6] à Londres.*
Although her literature is not to today's taste, the prose being overwrought and sentimental, it's certainly very pacy. Her characters tend to SHOUT![7] at each other in capitals and exclamations.	*Si ses œuvres littéraires, au style ampoulé et sentimental, sont aujourd'hui désuètes, elles ne manquent pas pour autant d'action. Ses personnages ont tendance à se parler en CRIANT! à grand renfort[7] de majuscules et d'exclamations.*
This style of gesticulatory melodrama went down a storm with Edwardians. Emma proved hugely popular and is still collected today in historical and mystery anthologies[8] of a more esoteric nature."	*Ce style mélodramatique et théâtral était très prisé à la Belle Époque. Emma Orczy connut un énorme succès et ses œuvres figurent encore aujourd'hui dans les anthologies historiques et policières[8] d'un genre plus ésotérique.*

BRIEF

The passage is to be translated for a French literary magazine featuring less well-known female authors.

MACRO STRATEGY

This is an extract from *The Book of Forgotten Authors* by Christopher Fowler, published in 2017. It gives a short profile of Emma Orczy, one of the "forgotten" authors presented in the book. There are cultural references to London (Great Portland Street), to British institutions (Scotland Yard, the Royal Academy) and to British history (the Edwardians), as well as references to Orczy's works. The language is informal, using contractions ("weren't"), abbreviations ("UK") and **idioms** ("go down a storm"). The vocabulary is standard with occasional "rarer" adjectives used to describe Orczy's style (e.g., "gesticulatory"). The passage appears to have been edited (second paragraph), and the overall effect is that of a series of facts rather than a cohesive whole. Cohesion is maintained through a repetition of the subject's name or surname and the relatively frequent use of the pronoun "she" and the possessive "her." The meaning of the piece is clear. Fowler provides selected biographical notes on Emma Orczy to give the reader an idea of her life and work. He sometimes presents the facts with a tinge of irony and humour. The author's subjectivity comes through in the chosen lexis ("she fetched up"), an apparent fondness for adverbs such as "certainly" and typographic features that aim at mimicking Orczy's style ("*SHOUT!*"). While the French translation needs to attempt to convey some of the informality of the style, it should not feel too informal or too "modern," and overall, it should have a more literary quality than the original in order to fit this type of publication. Some of the cultural references may need to be explained (e.g., Great Portland Street) or replaced (e.g., the Edward-ians → *la Belle Époque*) for the purpose of readability and to give the reader a clearer idea of the period, and official French titles of Orczy's works will need to be researched. Because the source text feels at times bitty and elliptical, cohesion may need enhancing and some ideas may require expanding in the French version.

MICRO STRATEGIES AND COMMENTS

[1] **Restructuring**: This long string of information about the subject reads better in French if its content is repositioned within the sentence; this rearrangement of the informational content, together with a transposition from "Hungarian-born" to *d'origine hongroise* (instead of *née en Hongrie*) makes for better flow and readability.

[2] *Lexis/register*: The verb "fetched up" suggests a final settlement after a period of travels and short stays abroad – and indeed sources tell us that Emma Orczy lived in Brussels and Paris before settling in London. It is difficult to reflect the informality of the verb without risking striking an overly familiar – and unsuitable – note by choosing a similarly colloquial French verb meaning to arrive somewhere, such as *atterrir à*. The more neutral *se retrouver à* was chosen, as it captures the idea of ending up somewhere.

[3] *Word order*: The word *London* is introduced earlier in the French version, just before the Great Portland Street address, as French readers outside Britain may not know which city that street is in. To avoid repetition, "London" has been replaced by a synonym (*la capitale britannique*) at the end of the first paragraph. It could be argued that the Great Portland Street address could be removed alto-gether in the French version, but the decision was taken to retain it to express a sense of place and of the exotic.

[4] *Tone*: There is a hint of humour and possibly an understatement in the nega-tive phrasing "there weren't too many occupations for a deposed baroness." In the French, a modulation from a negative to an affirmative statement conveys the idea of work scarcity, while the adjective *maigres* has a slightly sardonic undertone.

[5] *Pronouns*: Where Fowler uses the subject pronoun "she" or the possessive "her," the French translation chooses either to repeat "Emma Orczy" or to use an

alternative such as *la baronne Orczy* further on in the second paragraph. This is because the direct equivalents of "she" and "her" (*elle, son/ses/sa*) may appear weak cohesive devices to French readers, especially if used to start a paragraph, as the possessive "Her" is used in the English text. Using variations of the subject's name also feels more natural in French.

[6] *Proper nouns*: The references to Scotland Yard and the Royal Academy have been left untranslated, partly to retain the sense of foreign places in the French version but also because it is assumed that many readers interested in British literature and culture would be familiar with these two institutions.

[7] *Style*: The addition here of *à grand renfort de* clarifies Fowler's meaning and conveys more explicitly his humorous attempt, by way of the use of capitals, at bringing to life Orczy's florid style.

[8] *Lexis*: One of the challenges in this translation is to find equivalent terms for the literary genres mentioned in the source text, such as "mystery fiction" and "mystery anthologies." The terms *romans policiers* and *anthologies policières* were chosen here because they are clearly understood genres of fiction. In French literature, genres and sub-genres do not appear to be divided along the same lines as in British culture. In a French bookshop, for example, fiction will usually be divided into *littérature* (poetry, plays, paperbacks, and so on), on the one hand, and *polar, science-fiction* and *bandes dessinées*, on the other. The term *policier* seemed the most appropriate here. Incidentally, the term *polar*, widely used in French fiction typology, was not used in this translation – not because it is regarded as too familiar but because it was coined in the sixties and would therefore feel too "modern," and would thus be an **anachronism** in the context of Emma Orczy's work.

Source text 4 – English into Italian

From *Platform*, Vol. 11, "Authenticity," Autumn 2017 – *Jean Dubuffet & Art Brut: The Creation of an Avant-Garde Identity* by Antonia Dapena-Tretter.

"In search of a creative awakening like his artistic predecessors, Dubuffet made a series of trips to the French colony of Algeria[1] (1947–1949). He took with him pencils and paper to pass out to willing[2] natives in hopes of observing their art-making habits. Works created by Dubuffet either in Algeria, or from memory shortly thereafter, include a number of gouaches and oil paintings.	*Alla ricerca, come i suoi predecessori artistici, di uno stimolo creativo, Dubuffet intraprese una serie di viaggi (1947–1949) nella colonia francese di Algeria,[1] portando con sé carta e matite da distribuire agli indigeni disposti a collaborare,[2] nella speranza di poterne osservare le modalità di creazione artistica. Le opere create da Dubuffet durante il soggiorno in Algeria, o a memoria poco tempo dopo, comprendono alcune gouaches e dipinti ad olio.*

(Continued)

(Continued)

Apparently, the appeal proved attractive[3] in concept only. . . . In 1949 he officially declared: "I have for the moment renounced the descriptive arts of exoticisms." By excluding "exoticisms," the artist had eliminated the possibility of finding inspiration in geographic or ethnic difference. In doing so, Dubuffet purposefully restricted his search for the primitive to the people living in his own Western culture.	*A quanto pare l'attrattiva si rivelò tale[3] solo a livello teorico. . . . Nel 1949 Dubuffet dichiarò ufficialmente: "Per ora ho rinunciato alle arti descrittive dell'esotismo."* *Escludendo "l'esotismo," l'artista aveva scartato la possibilità di trovare ispirazione nella diversità geografica od etnica e, così facendo, limitò di proposito la propria ricerca della primitività alle popolazioni che vivevano in seno alla sua stessa cultura occidentale.*
This new otherness was harder to delineate. It required Dubuffet to coin the term Art Brut[4] and then to define its parameters. This first iteration of the category was very much an umbrella term[5] to describe all sorts of marginal art, including art from asylums, folk art, self-taught masters, drawings by children, tattoos, graffiti, and even cave paintings.	*Questo nuovo tipo di alterità era più difficile da delineare, tanto che Dubuffet si trovò a dover coniare il termine Art Brut[4] e successivamente a definirne i parametri. Questa prima iterazione della categoria era sostanzialmente un termine onnicomprensivo[5] per descrivere arte marginale di tutti i tipi, tra cui arte proveniente da manicomi, arte popolare, maestri autodidatti, disegni fatti da bambini, tatuaggi, graffiti e persino pitture rupestri.*
Realizing that the term was a bit vague, Dubuffet wrote in a 1945 letter: "Naturally, Art Brut is very difficult to define without getting confused. . . . But there is no reason for saying that something does not exist because it is elusive and indefinable." The word "elusive" suggests that the artist meant not only to define Art Brut but to capture it.	*Realizzando che il termine era un po' vago, Dubuffet scrisse, in una lettera del 1945: "L'Art Brut è senza dubbio molto difficile da definire senza confondersi. . . . Ma non vedo perché si debba dire che una cosa non esiste solo per il fatto che è sfuggente e indefinibile."* *Il termine "sfuggente" suggerisce che l'artista intendesse non solo definire l'Art Brut ma anche catturarla.*
He would own this slippery category, pinning it more firmly into position with each definition, and by the time Dubuffet arranged his first exhibition of the newly-formed collection, he revealed a noticeably narrowed focus."	*Dubuffet avrebbe fatto sua questa categoria inafferrabile, inchiodandola sempre più saldamente al proprio posto, una definizione dopo l'altra, tanto che, quando arrivò ad organizzare la prima mostra della neonata collezione, rivelò un campo d'azione decisamente ristretto.*

BRIEF

The text is a sample for an academic publisher, which intends to commission a translation of a book on Dubuffet.

MACRO STRATEGY

The pre-translation phase for this high-register academic text required extensive research into a specialised topic. Reading and understanding the full article from which the extract was taken was essential, especially in terms of extra-textual references; this enabled the translator to detect a somewhat critical stance towards Dubuffet, which sets the tone of the ST.

Several **model texts** were consulted and analysed for terminology and register.

An educated and specialist audience was assumed, in possession of enough extra-textual knowledge for glosses to be avoided and a high TT register maintained, as well as a complex structure.

However, as the sentence structure of the ST was often dense, several recasting operations were used to achieve a transparent and natural-sounding TT.

MICRO STRATEGIES

[1] *Grammar/syntax*: SL conventions allow for a typically paratactic style, where clauses are placed beside each other with minimal use of conjunctions. Conversely, the target language adopts a typically hypotactic writing style, favouring the subordination of clauses, especially in academic, high-register writing.

The punctuation was altered here, by joining the two sentences with a comma and turning the past simple into a gerundive (i.e. He took with him = *portando con se*), which is more in line with the source text's style of academic writing. The same operation was carried out later in the text: ("... harder to delineate. It required Dubuffet...").

[2] *Grammar/expansion*: "Willing natives": the term "willing" used attributively before the noun means "disposed to do what is required" or "ready to be of use or service." The target language needs to place the translation of "willing" (*disposto*) in a predicative position (i.e., *indigeni disposti a*). Therefore, the source text is expanded with the use of a subordinate clause *(disposto) a collaborare)*.

[3] *Reduction*: "The appeal proved attractive": the encoding of "appeal" and "attractive" requires the same word in the TL (*attrattiva/attraente*) or very close synonyms. To avoid tautology, "attractive" has been omitted and replaced by the strategic use of **anaphora** (i.e., *tale*).

[4] **Direct transfer**: *Art Brut* (context-specific term): This term refers to the art movement created by Dubuffet; the definition has been adopted as such by the international art community and is assumed to be understood by the educated (specialist) TT audience. Several model texts of equivalent style and register were checked to confirm suitability of choice. The same strategy applied to "gouaches," a linguistic import from French, which is also used in Italian, although sometimes encoded as *guazzi*.

[5] **Sense translation**: "Umbrella term" is a compound that is not easy to replicate in Italian; the sense has been preserved by using a corresponding generic adjective for "umbrella" (*onnicomprensivo*).

> **Pause for thought**: If you translate from English into French, German, Italian or Spanish, choose one of the preceding translations and provide three extra annotations, commenting on the translator's choices.

2ii: Texts from French, German, Italian and Spanish into English

This part contains source texts from French, German, Italian and Spanish translated into English, with some translations specifically commissioned for this book from a representative selection of literary and semi-literary sources. As in Part 2i, each translation is accompanied by a macro strategy and about six micro strategies with comments, showing how the translation challenges have been approached and resolved.

French text

The following passage is taken from Patrick Rotman's *Un Homme à Histoires*, a novel about incidents involving François Mitterrand and other politicians in the late 1950s at the time of the fall of French Indochina and the start of the Algerian war. This novel is particularly pertinent to the issues of time and context, since it was published in 2016 but purports to have been written in the mid-1970s about the 1950s. The extract that follows contains some useful writing tips given to a trainee reporter by Françoise Giroud on how to write a piece in the *L'Express* house style.

"'Un article, ce n'est pas une dissertation, encore moins une thèse. Il y a des livres pour ça.[1] Le journalisme, c'est superficiel, c'est léger, ça se déguste vite[2] et s'oublie encore plus vite. Le lendemain,[3] votre prose sert à emballer les poireaux. Vous aimez les poireaux?'

Tout en parlant, Françoise Giroud s'était mise à raturer à grands coups de stylo rouge les feuilles commises[4] par la jeune femme blonde, qui, d'une main, caressait la frange impeccable de ses cheveux dorés. Le verdict tomba, sévère.

"'An article is not a dissertation, let alone a thesis. If that's what people want,[1] they can read books. Journalism scrapes the surface, it's light, it's fast food,[2] and is forgotten even faster. The day after publication,[3] your work will be used to wrap up a bunch of leeks. Do you like leeks?'

As she spoke, Françoise Giroud started to make thick strokes with a red pen through the offending copy submitted[4] by the young blonde, who was running the fingers of one hand through the perfectly styled fringe in her golden hair. The verdict was delivered, a tough one.

'Trop long,[5] beaucoup trop long, Solange. Un article doit toucher6 le lecteur à la première phrase. Cela ne sert à rien d'avoir du talent à la dixième ligne si le lecteur ne dépasse pas la troisième. Il vous faut recommencer, plus concis, plus direct. Et puis éviter les relatives sans objet et les circonstancielles où le lecteur s'égare.

Qu'est-ce qu'ils vous ont appris à la Sorbonne? Ce n'est pas pourtant pas sorcier d'écrire une phrase en français: sujet, verbe, complément, pas d'adverbe. Évitez être et avoir. Rayer les adjectifs!"

'It's[5] too long, far too long, Solange. An article must hook[6] the reader with the first sentence. It's no good having talent in the tenth line if the reader doesn't read beyond the third. You must start again; be more concise, more to the point. And avoid relative clauses without a complement and circumstantial clauses where the reader loses track.

What did they teach you at the Sorbonne? You don't have to be a magician to be able write a sentence in French: It's just subject, verb, complement, and no adverbs. Avoid 'to be' and 'to have' and cross out the adjectives!"

BRIEF

Having read this novel while on holiday in France, you have obtained the translation rights for this novel from the French publisher and now you need to prepare a translation sample to send out to prospective UK publishers.

MACRO STRATEGY

It proved useful to have read the entire book because this provided a wider context and demonstrated the need to maintain the correct register and viewpoint. Much of the novel is written in the first person as a fictitious memoir, but this extract features the unequal relationship between an experienced editor and a trainee journalist and is reported in dialogue form as a conversation overheard by the main protagonist. To ensure that the **tenor** was captured correctly, UK websites were searched for parallel texts containing writing tips for trainee journalists, and advice given to family members who trained as journalists in the 1970s and '80s was also considered. One conversation recollected from a journalists' training course contained a put-down similar to that in the French source text:

> Course tutor: "No sentence should be more than 30 words long."
> Trainee journalist: "But this sentence by Bernard Levin is 96 words long."
> Course tutor: "You can only say that when **you** can write like Bernard Levin."

A further parallel text that was helpful when researching the contextual and cultural background of the time was Philip Short's 2013 biography *Mitterrand* (London: Bodley Head), which shed further light on the factual basis for Rotman's account of these turbulent times.

MICRO STRATEGIES AND COMMENTS

[1] *Expansion*: The source text has been expanded to make the message more coherent: it would sound too abrupt in English.

[2] *Metaphor and meaning*: The first draft was *it's a quick taster*, but this was rejected because it changes the meaning, implying there is more to follow. Another option the translator considered was *it's ephemeral*, because she had heard British journalists describing the nature of their work in this way. This rendering would have meant that "encore plus vite" would have been meaningless if the concept of speed contained in "vite" had been eliminated.

[3] *Context*: An obvious rendering here would be *tomorrow*, but this was rejected because of the contextual information given two pages earlier in the novel, which explained that *L'Express* was the Saturday supplement of a paper called *Les Échos*. Short's biography proved that both these publications actually existed, as did their founders.

[4] *Implied meaning*: The ST uses "les feuilles commises" rather than a more standard collocation, such as "les feuilles soumises," thus introducing negative overtones suggesting that the new recruit has committed an offence by handing in inferior work.

[5] *Ellipsis in the source text*: A subject and a verb have been inserted here to improve coherence, because there is a natural pause between what Françoise Giroud has just said and her final comments to explain what is wrong with Solange's article.

[6] *Equivalence of context*: A slight over-translation seems justifiable here. Although *hook* is much stronger than the ST "toucher," it was a deliberate choice because "to hook the reader" is a collocation almost always used by creative writing tutors in an equivalent UK context (see Chapter 4).

German text

BRIEF

The following passage is an extract taken from *Der Schabbes*, a description of the traditional celebration of the *Shabbes*, which appeared in Israel A. Glück's memoir *Kindheit in Lackenbach*, published in 1998 by Hartung-Gorre Verlag in Konstanz and edited by Erhard R. Wiehn. It recreates a vanished world – village life in a Jewish community in the Austrian state of Burgenland at the time of the Austro-Hungarian empire. The translation is to appear in an anthology of Jewish historical memoirs to be published in the UK.

"Nach ein paar ereignislosen Tagen begannen die Vorbereitungen. [1]Bereits am Mittwoch herrschte in Haus und Küche regere Tätigkeit, die sich am Donnerstag noch verstärkte. Im Waschtrog wurde aus Weizenmehl[2] Teig geknetet, zu großen 'Barches'[3] (Zopfbrote) geflochten, die man dann zum Bäcker schickte.

"After a few uneventful days, the preparations began. In the house and the kitchen there was already more lively activity by Wednesday,[1] and this intensified on Thursday. Dough made from wheat flour[2] was kneaded in the washtub, and plaited into large Challah,[3] which were then sent to the baker's.

Aber am Freitag erreichte das 'Schabbesmachen' seinen Höhepunkt. Schon frühmorgens brutzelte es in den Töpfen am Herd, Mitzi[4] schleppte Eimer um Eimer mit Wasser vom Brunnen – hier gab es keinen Wasserhahn im Haus wie in der Stadt.

Es wurde gefegt, gespült, gewaschen, geputzt, gebürstet, gewischt. Wir Kinder standen natürlich überall im Weg. Schickte man uns in den Garten, waren wir gleich wieder im Haus – der allgemeine Rummel zog uns an wie ein Magnet. Bis[5] Mama auf die blendende Idee kam, uns mit einem Stückchen Schokolade zu bestechen. Das wirket eine Weile, dann standen wir wieder im Weg – bis zur nächsten Bestechung.

Freitag mittag schloß Großpapa sein Geschäft, nahm ein Bündel frischer Wäsche[6] und ein großes Handtuch unter den Arm und ging zur 'Mikwe' – ins Ritualbad.

Wir Kinder wurden zu Hause im Waschtrog gebadet, schön gekämmt und 'schabbesdig' gekleidet. Mama beschwor mich jedesmal, auf meinen sauberen Schabbes-Anzug aufzupassen, doch ungeachtet meines feierlichen Versprechens und der allerbesten Vorsätze passierte mir immer irgend etwas."

But on Friday the 'Shabbes-making' reached its peak. By early morning, pots were bubbling away on the stove, Mitzi (the maid[4]) fetched bucket after bucket of water from the well – there was no tap here like in the town.

Things were swept, rinsed out, washed, cleaned, brushed, wiped down. We children constantly got in the way, of course. If they sent us into the garden, we were back in the house straight away – the general hustle and bustle attracted us like a magnet. That is,[5] until Mum came up with the brilliant idea of bribing us with a piece of chocolate. That worked for a while, and then we got in the way again – until the next bribe was produced.

Friday lunchtimes, Grandfather shut up his shop, took a bundle of fresh underwear[6] and a large towel under his arm and went to the mikvah for a ritual bath.

We children were bathed at home in the washtub, our hair was nicely combed and we were dressed in our Shabbes clothes. Every time Mother implored me to mind my clean Shabbes suit, yet in spite of my solemn promise and my very best intentions, something always happened to me."

MACRO STRATEGY

It seemed essential to ensure that the cultural and religious terms were appropriate, so a practising British Jew was consulted about the most acceptable spellings, which could not be found in a standard dictionary such as *Collins English Dictionary & Thesaurus 21st Century Edition*. Online searches revealed a number of conflicting spellings. It appears that Ashkenazi Jews might use the Yiddish word *Shabbos*, still current in more orthodox religious groups in the UK, whereas younger Jews, Sephardi Jews and Israelis would use the modern Hebrew version *Shabbat*. Parallel texts were studied to see how other translators had dealt with this issue. A translation of a sample chapter from a similar book, *Scenes of Jewish Village Life in Alsace: Village Tales from 19th-Century France* written by Auguste Widal in 1860, is published on US translator Steven Capsuto's blog. Here an initial reference was found to "Shabbes – the Sabbath" and thereafter just "the Sabbath." A search through works by Jewish writers revealed a character referring to "Shabbes" in Howard Jacobson's *Kalooki Nights* published by Vintage Books in London (2007: 53). However, Nicholas de Lange's translation from Hebrew of Amos Oz's "Scenes from Village Life," which features stories set in Israel, uses "Sabbath."

A decision then had to be made as to whether to opt for a modern translation using Hebrew-derived terminology, such as *preparing for Shabbat/Shabbat preparations*, or to retain the period feel of the piece and use Yiddish-based terms. Because this is a memoir, the latter seemed more appropriate to the culture in a Jewish village at that time, which led to the choice of the spelling *Shabbes*.

MICRO STRATEGIES AND COMMENTS

[1] *Coherence*: The relative pronoun *which* needs to be close to its referent, so the English sentence cannot begin with *By Wednesday*. The original version included two consecutive adverbial phrases: *By Wednesday, in the house and in the kitchen*, which was resolved by placing *by Wednesday* just before the relative clause. It then seemed better to eliminate the relative clause altogether and use the co-ordinating conjunction *and*, followed by *this*. It is also stylistically more pleasing because it avoids repetition, given that *which* appears in the next sentence.

[2] *Word order*: For the sake of coherence, the expression "aus Weizenmehl" has been moved further away from the verb "wurde geknetet," and a past participle, *made from*, has been inserted.

[3] *Lexis*: To avoid the tautology *plaited into plaited loaves*, the better-known term *challah* was used rather than *Barches*, which seems to be confined to the German-speaking world. An explanation or gloss was then no longer necessary. For the US market, *plaited* might need to be replaced by *braided*.

[4] *Expansion*: Contextual information was added to clarify the identity of Mitzi, which would not be clear to someone reading this extract out of context.

[5] *Ellipsis*: To improve **clarity**, the ellipsis in the source text was compensated for by inserting a dummy subject and verb *That is*.

[6] *Meaning*: "Wäsche" is polysemic and could be rendered with *washing, laundry* or *linen* or even *clothes*, but from the context, the implied meaning appears to be *underwear*, with "Wäsche" having one of its secondary meanings, that of "Unterwäsche."

Italian text

The following Italian passage is another extract from the short story *Tornare nelle Murge* by Carlo Castellaneta (1990: 38), in which the narrator returns to the land of his birth, in Italy's "deep south."

"Ormai non passavano più asinelli, come lui ne ricordava al trotto verso il crepuscolo, col contadino seduto di fianco sulla groppa che gli ballavano le gambe,[1] ma solo automobili o camion che parevano inseguiti da qualcuno, tanto si avventavano giù nella discesa,[2] ed era bello starsene lì con la Mercedes bianca di polvere, come uno straniero con la targa del Nord tra i fichidindia.

E pensare che fino a uno, due anni prima, se gliel'avessero chiesto avrebbe potuto scommetterci sopra: che quaggiù non avrebbe più messo piede, talmente si sentiva[3] estranea e remota la terra d'origine, un nome sui documenti e nient'altro. Invece negli ultimi tempi si era insinuato dentro di lui un sentimento strano, che non era nostalgia né rimorso, ma qualcosa di impreciso che comunuque si era sostituito[4] all'ostilità con cui aveva sempre pensato alle sue radici, al punto da rimuoverle come se non fossero esistite.

– O Cristo, sono cicale! – pensò ad alta voce. E si rivide bambino con una verde cicala che gli schizzava fuori dal pugno appena aveva aperto la mano.

[5]Adesso il concerto pareva un respiro della terra, la vibrazione saliva dal mare giallo degli steli riarsi fino a rendere tremolante l'orizzonte che l'uomo fissava come inebetito,[6] era un presenza possente e invisibile."

"There were no donkeys anymore. He remembered them trotting by as the light fell, with a peasant sitting sideways on the animal's back, his legs dangling.[1] But now there were just cars or lorries, careering down the slope, as if they were being chased.[2] It was wonderful to be there in the Mercedes, white with dust, like a foreigner with a Northern registration among the prickly-pears.

And to think that a couple of years ago, if anyone had asked him, he would have sworn never to go back there, so foreign and remote was the land of his birth to him[3] – nothing more than a place in his passport. But recently a strange feeling had taken hold of him – neither nostalgia nor remorse, rather something hard to define that had melted[4] the hostility he felt towards his roots – and so much so, it seemed that these feelings had never existed.

"Good Heavens, they're cicadas!" he exclaimed. And there he was, a child again, with a green cicada leaping from his clenched fist as soon as he opened his hand.

[5]Now the concert resounded as if the very earth were breathing, the vibration rising through the yellow sea of dried stalks up to the trembling horizon – a presence at once powerful and invisible, which he stared at in wonderment.[6]"

BRIEF

The story from which this excerpt is taken is for publication in a collection of short stories about southern Europe, titled "Deep South."

MACRO STRATEGY

The main challenge in this passage is to create the same impressions on the target reader as those on the source text reader. The impressions are not just visual but also sensory and emotive. Achieving the same effect requires changes to the language and sentence structure, to build a convincing and holistic representation in the target language of both what is happening and what is experienced. The timeframe/context progresses from snapshots of the past to a final, almost surreal, dimension.

MICRO STRATEGIES AND COMMENTS

[1] *Structure*: This very long sentence, with its rolling sequence of impressions, has been cut into four shorter ones, in order to create more clearly defined images.

[2] *Sequence*: The order has been reversed to emphasise the vehicles rushing down the slope and the impression this has on the narrator. This seems a more logical way of "painting the picture" in English.

[3] *Emphasis* is retained by using a similar mechanism in English to "talmente" but with the removal of "si sentiva," as a specific translation of this verb would complicate the sentence structure. Moreover, there are several other references in the text to the narrator's feelings and state of mind.

[4] *Lexis*: A literal translation of "si era sostituito" would sound banal in this poetic context, so a more figurative form was used.

[5] *Description*: The noise of the cicadas resounds and vibrates, creating a mystical and primal effect on the narrator. His impressions have been "visualised" to create a similar effect on the target language reader.

[6] *Emphasis*: The reference to the narrator's amazement is delayed until the very end of the sentence, in order to separate the description from the emotion it generates, rather than embed it in the discourse.

(South American) Spanish text

The Spanish text is taken from the second chapter of the e-book *Entre aquí y allá* by Claudia Forero, a Latin American writer, published in London by *El Ojo De la Cultura Hispanoamericana* (2017: 100).

Apaguemos	*Let's turn off the lights*
"Diecisiete de septiembre de 1986 en Fonseca,[1] capital de La Republica.[1] Nos encontramos en ese espacio de tiempo que queda entre una y otra edición, se aproxima el final de la tarde y el principio de la noche,[2] muchos periodistas ya se han marchado.	"*September 17th, 1986. Fonseca,[1] capital of La Republica.[1] We are in the period of time that elapses between one edition and the next; evening's ending, it's nearly nightfall.[2] Many journalists have already left.*
Es el momento de conversar, ir a mirar la información de las agencias, pasar por la rotativa,[3] tomar un café, comer algo, antes de la otra edición.	*It's time to have a chat, glance at the latest from the news agencies, check the printing press,[3] grab a coffee and a bite to eat before the next edition.*

Apaguemos	Let's turn off the lights
Él salió como llegaba en las mañanas. Caminando suave, como un gato, sonriéndole a la gente como un papá, como quien se asegura que todo en casa esté bien. Después ya nunca más volvió.	He left, just like he arrived every morning, stepping softly, like a cat, smiling at the people like a father, like someone satisfying himself that all's well at home. Afterwards, he never came back.
Hoy, apenas días después, miramos desde arriba, desde nuestra sala de redacción, la entrada del féretro y detrás toda la gente que lo amaba.[4] Vemos al director, o mejor ya no lo vemos, solo lo presentimos en su ataúd. Ese féretro visto desde la redacción pasa ante nuestros ojos como si volara y se hiciera más grande, nos cuesta hablar, tal vez sentimos lo mismo: dolor, desesperanza, desolación.[5]	Today, only days afterwards, up in the editorial office, we are gazing down upon his coffin as it enters, with all the people who loved him[4] following behind. We see our Editor, or rather we no longer see him, we only sense his presence in the coffin which, seen from above, passes before our eyes, seeming to soar and becoming much larger. Words fail us, though perhaps our feelings are the same: despondency, despair, desolation.[5]
Nos percibimos solos; solos sin él, solos en el país y solos con nosotros mismos. Siento que estamos en verdadero duelo, en nuestro periódico que olemos y respiramos y sentimos todos los días. Todo parece que me llega y me golpea la cara, el estómago, las vísceras. 'La facilidad con la que se asesina' me repito en silencio."[6]	We feel so alone: alone without him, alone in this country, alone even amongst ourselves. I sense that we are in genuine mourning here, where we eat, sleep and breathe the newspaper. Everything seems to assail me: a sharp blow to my face, my stomach, my heart. "Murder is so easily done," I say silently to myself.[6]"

BRIEF

This extract is to be translated for potential publication in an anthology of work by members of a writing group based in Surrey.

MACRO STRATEGY

This brief excerpt is carefully composed and atmospheric. It encompasses an entire gamut of emotions described by the narrator, who is young at the time in which the passage is set (1986). The focus of the passage changes from broad expression of contentment in the first paragraph to individual expression of grief at the end of the final one. The translation aims to reflect the youth of the narrator and to voice her situation, experience and feelings appropriately. It seemed inappropriate to tie this text down to a particular place or "domesticate" it, as emotion is universal. An effort has been made to render the musicality in the source text.

MICRO STRATEGIES AND COMMENTS

[1] *Proper nouns*: "Fonseca" and "La Republica." Transferring the names of the fictitious city and country, by writing the names in the target text exactly as they appear in the source text, is a deliberate strategy, as the reader will easily identify the word "Republica," while names of cities are usually left in the original form (unless there is a standard version of the name in the target language). Creating a "false" English city or country would be unnecessary "domestication."

[2] *Poetic effect*: *Evening's ending, it's nearly nightfall*: alliteration is employed here, avoiding *evening is nigh* or a similar archaic phrase – to show that the translation is a product of its time and reflect the young narrator's voice. The contractions are deliberate here: the register in the first part of this passage is relatively low, reflecting the relaxed atmosphere at the end of the day and in sharp contrast to the higher register used in paragraph 3 to convey the solemn atmosphere after the death of the Editor.

[3] *Lexis*: *Printing press*/"la rotativa": the hyponym *rotary printer* or *rotary printing press* would be used in a technical translation, but given the literary genre, the superordinate (or broader term) *printing press* is more appropriate. It is also alliterative and evocative of whirring and clicking (see reference to musicality in the Macro Strategy).

[4] *Lexis*: *All the people who loved him*: Avoidance of cliché here, such as *his nearest and dearest* or *his kith and kin* on the basis that this would move the text too much into the target culture.

[5] *Alliteration* in the source text with repetition of "d" (dolor, desesperanza, desolación) is reflected in the target text and aims to evoke the tolling of a bell. "Dolor" is commonly translated *pain* or *grief*, but alliteration was accorded more importance than using standard equivalents in English; *dolorous* and *doleful* were considered but rejected, on the basis that *dolorous* is archaic and therefore would be "marked" and sound "jarring" in the mouth of the young narrator, while *doleful* often has connotations of *peeved* or *disappointed* and is therefore inappropriate in context.

[6] *Meaning*: The translator's original rendering was *"Murder is so simple," I say silently to myself*: "Se asesina" (literally "one assassinates") would suggest that the victim was a politician (cf Martin Luther King Jr. or John F. Kennedy), and whether or not the killing was politically motivated, *murder* is an appropriate choice in context. *The ease with which one commits a murder* sounded stilted, so emphasis was created with *murder* by placing this harsh word at the start of the sentence and then creating a soft ending to the piece. The sibilance of repeated "s" sounds ("c" in "facilidad" and "silencio" can be pronounced "s," giving the sounds "fasilidad" "se" "asesina" "silensio"), a technique which was replicated in the target text. After consultation with the author of the Spanish source text, who felt that *simple* did not quite replicate the intended meaning, this word was changed to *easily done*, retaining both the sibilance and the context of the culture of killing. She added that the motive for the murder described in this story was, in fact, political.

> **Pause for thought**: If you translate from French, German, Italian or Spanish into English, choose one of the preceding translations and provide three extra comments on the translator's choices.

PART 3: TRANSLATION COMPARISONS

Comparisons of translations can be approached in different ways, for example:

1   By comparing one target text with the source text, using analytical and/or qualitative criteria;
2   By comparing two (or more) target texts with each other and with the source text, using analytical and/or qualitative criteria.

Using *analytical criteria* for comparison (*see* our model, pp. 57–60) represents a *factual approach* to analysis, by identifying specific textual features of relevance to the translation process and then observing how the translator has approached the task and resolved the challenges it poses. In contrast, *qualitative criteria* involve judging the *success* of a translation, both in terms of the accurate and appropriate holistic rendering of the source text but also as a piece of writing in its own right. Marking criteria and guidelines specifically designed to assess the translator's competence, in terms of the accuracy and appropriateness of the translation and the quality of the target language, are widely used to assess undergraduate and postgraduate translation assignments and exams, or in professional qualifications, such as the Chartered Institute of Linguists' *Diploma in Translation*, where the benchmark for translation acceptability is "to be deemed professionally usable," calculated on a points system (IoL Educational Trust, "Diploma in Translation – Marking Guidelines").

These models assess translations set for a specific academic – or professional – purpose, but there are other approaches to quality, as Sonia Colina points out in the chapter "Translation Quality" in *Fundamentals of Translation* (2015, Cambridge University Press). She mentions **reader response approaches**, derived from work by Nida, Taber and Carroll in the 1960s, which assess "the quality of the translation by determining whether readers of the translation respond to it as readers of the source would respond to the original" (2015: 228). Another approach is "to assess the quality of the translation with respect to text type and function" – an approach that resembles our analytical model, as it looks at textual and situational features in the source and target texts, compares the two and then forms an opinion of the result, based on whether "the textual profile and function of the translation match those of the original, the goal being the *functional equivalence* between the original and the translation." The merit of textual approaches, according to Colina, is that they "have made a significant contribution . . . by shifting the focus from counting errors at the word or sentence level to evaluating entire texts and goals of translation, giving the reader and communication a much more prominent role" (2015: 229).

A translation assessment process is ideally a holistic process, which takes into account the textual features of the source text but also the background to the text, the purpose and intended use of the translation (where such details are known), the specific or assumed readership and the cultural context in which it will be disseminated. To make the analytical process interactive, we provide prompts through the Questions, to generate a response and enhance the communication process.

In Part 3, comparison of source/target texts focuses on both the general approach to the translation task and specific translation choices.

The first comparison involves three translations, published in 1924, 1961 and 1995, of extracts from *Les Liaisons Dangéreuses* by Choderlos de Laclos, first published in the original French version in 1782. The French edition used here is published by Le Grand Livre du Mois (1993).

COMPARISON 1: French into English

Translation details

T1: *Les Liaisons Dangereuses*, Penguin Classics, translated by P. W. K. Stone (1961);

T2: *Les Liaisons Dangereuses*, Oxford World's Classics, translated by Douglas Parmée (1995);

(For the third translation, see the "Pause for thought" box following the comments on the Letter XV example).

From Letter I

Example Ta) Cécile Volanges to Sophie Carnay

Cécile and Sophie had become friends at a convent. Cécile writes to Sophie about what has been happening in her life since she left the convent. After starting the letter, she breaks off when called by her mother ('Adieu, jusqu'à un petit moment'). Example Ta) starts when Cécile resumes her letter.

Example Tb)

Letter 1 continues with a description of a gentleman arriving at the house. Cécile's embarrassment is due to mistaking him for a potential suitor approved by her mother, only to find that he has simply come to measure her for some shoes. On realising her mistake, Cécile describes her reactions.

From Letter XV

Example Tc)

In this example, the libertine Vicomte de Valmont writes to his former lover, the Marquise de Merteuil, who – to amuse herself – is urging him to seduce Cécile.

Source text	Penguin Classics version, translated by P. W. K. Stone in 1961	Oxford World's Classics version, translated by Douglas Parmée in 1995
Example Ta): "Comme tu vas te moquer de la pauvre Cécile ! Oh ! j'ai été bien honteuse ! Mais tu y aurais été attrapée comme moi."	**T1:** *"How you will laugh at your poor Cécile! I was so ashamed of myself! But you would have been caught just as I was."*	**T2:** *"Here I am again and you're really going to laugh at me! It's ever so embarrassing but you'd have been taken in just as much as me."*
Example Tb): "Ta pauvre Cécile alors a perdu la tête; j'étais, comme a dit Maman, tout effarouchée. Je me suis levée en jetant un cri perçant; tiens, comme ce jour de tonnerre."	**T1:** *"Upon which I lost my head; I was, as Mamma said, utterly panic-stricken. I jumped up uttering a piercing shriek . . . just as I did that day there was a thunderstorm, do you remember?"*	**T2:** *"Poor me! I lost my head completely, as Mummy said, I was scared out of my wits and I leapt up with a scream, you know, just like that time there was that thunderclap."*
Example Tc): "Tenez, ma belle amie, tant que vous vous partagez entre plusieurs, je n'ai la moindre jalousie: je ne vois alors dans vos amants que les successeurs d'Alexandre, incapables de conserver entre eux tous cet empire où je regnais seul."	**T1:** *"The fact is, my love, that as long as you distribute your favours in more than one quarter I am not in the least jealous: your lovers remind me of Alexander's successors, unable to maintain between them that mighty empire where I once reigned alone."*	**T2:** *"Hark ye, fair lady: as long as you distribute your favours, I am not jealous in the least; I perceive your lovers purely as the successors of Alexander the Great: incompetent joint rulers of an empire where I once ruled supreme."*

Comments

The two translations show different approaches to *Viewpoint*: **T1** adheres closely to the ST (reflecting Peter Newmark's *semantic* translation), while **T2** is more communicative, with a bias towards the target culture (*domestication*). The *Time* question in the analytical model asks how the timeframes affect the translation process, which is relevant to certain target language choices here, given the date of the book and the time gap between the dates of the translations. *Context* is also of particular importance, because of Cécile's misunderstanding. *Culture* is reflected in the references "Alexandre" and "Maman," which are treated differently by the translators.

Example Ta)

1   **T1** retains the original sentence structure, while **T2** merges sentences 2 and 3. The cohesion and coherence are more effective in **T2**.
2   **T1** reflects the source text register (as far as possible, given the differences between the two languages) and sounds a bit stilted, while **T2** uses a very colloquial register ("ever so embarrassing") including contracted verb forms, such as "you'd."
3   In terms of meaning, in **T1**, the literal translation of "attrapée" (*caught*) is ambiguous and *caught **out*** would have made more sense; "attrapée" does not have a physical connotation here and seems an attempt to create suspense, to make Cécile's misunderstanding of the situation all the more surprising (*see Example Tb*). **T2** has *taken in*, but as this phrase implies deliberately misleading someone (not the case here), it appears inappropriate.

Pause for thought: What is your preferred translation for "attrapée" in context? Give your reasons.

Example Tb)

1   **T1** structure follows the same fragmentary pattern as the ST yet remains coherent; in an effort to improve the flow, **T2** causes ambiguity with *as Mummy said*, which could refer to either "a perdu la tête" or "j'étais ... tout effarouchée."
2   The translation of "Maman" is relevant throughout the book, as Cécile's mother is referred to frequently in her daughter's letters. **T1** has *Mamma* (rather than the more common spelling *Mama*). The use of *Mummy* (**T2**) appears too modern for the eighteenth century timeframe/context; there is a need to respect the **politeness** and address code that applied in high society at the time, and *Mummy* simply sounds out of place. Even by the early twentieth century, boys from the upper (and sometimes middle) classes would address their parents as *Sir* and *Mother* or *Mama*.
3   The translation of "ce jour de tonnerre" in both versions suggests that a literal translation may not work: "ce jour" implies the girls' shared experience, and both translators resort to **paraphrase** to render the idea. **T1** translates the

phrase as *the day there was a thunderstorm* (to convey the idea of "jour" as well as "tonnerre") and **T2** as *the time there was that thunderclap* (focusing on the single loud noise that startles Cécile).

Pause for thought: Which of the preceding versions do you think is the better solution for "ce jour de tonnerre" in context? Can you think of a better way of expressing the phrase?

Example Tc)

1 **T2** tends to be communicative in approach but uses an archaism to translate "Tenez, ma belle amie" (i.e., *Hark ye, fair lady*), which may serve to remind readers of the historical setting or to reinforce Valmont's sarcasm (or both). The register has shifted from colloquial in Ta) and Tb) to rhetorical in Tc). The difference in register in **T1**'s version is less marked.

2 **T2** specifies *Alexander the Great*, using a domestication strategy, where the translator assumes a knowledge gap and localises the item by supplying extra information to the readership.

These examples highlight differences in approach and translation decision-making. **T1** generally shows greater deference towards the "author's voice," and by following the source text closely (though not necessarily always pedantically) suggests the time of the novel through the use of language. While **T2** may be easier to follow for a present-day reader, modern colloquial usage does not reflect the period or setting. It is interesting to note that some modern and contemporary authors, whose works are set in a historical context, deliberately choose a form of discourse designed to evoke "period" language. However, this tactic may be a distraction for the reader, unless it is done with a very light touch, and may end up verging on pastiche or parody.

Pause for thought: An earlier translation of the book (by Richard Aldington in 1924, published by Routledge) offers the following translations:

> **Ta)**: *How you will laugh at your poor Cécile! Oh! I was very much ashamed, but you would have been as helpless as I was.*

> **Tb)**: *Your poor Cécile then lost her head; as Mamma said, I was thoroughly scared. I sprang up with a piercing cry . . . just like the day of the thunderstorm.*

> **Tc)**: *Come, my fair friend, as long as you share yourself between several, I am not in the least jealous; I simply see your lovers as the successors*

> *of Alexander, incapable of holding among them all that Empire where I reigned alone.*

Now produce what you consider to be the optimal version of a), b) and c), drawing on the three translations to make a composite version. Then answer these questions:

1   Which of the three translations did you use the most? Why?
2   Which of the three translations did you use the least or not at all? Why?
3   How important were time and context factors in your version?
4   What strategy did you adopt with regard to "period language"?

COMPARISON 2: Italian into English from *I promessi sposi* by Alessandro Manzoni; the Italian version published by RCS Rizzoli Libri S.p.A., Milan, BUR 12th ed., 2011: 42–43). (The definitive Italian edition was published in 1840.)

Translation details

The Betrothed, Alessandro Manzoni, Penguin Books, London (translation by Bruce Penman, 1972: 33).

This famous passage occurs near the beginning of the book, set in 1628 by Lake Como; the Curé Don Abbondio is due to marry a young couple, Renzo Tramaglino and Lucia Mondella, but he is confronted while walking by two bravoes (henchmen of Don Rodrigo, the local lord). Northern Italy was under Spanish rule at this time.

Source text	Target text
"Signor Curato," disse un di que' due, piantandogli gli occhi in faccia.	"Your Reverence!" said one of them, staring him straight in the eyes.
"Cosa comanda?" rispose subito Don Abbondio, alzando i suoi occhi dal libro, che gli restò spalancato nelle mani, come sur un leggio.	"What can I do for you?" replied Don Abbondio immediately, looking up from his book, which remained open in his hands, as if on a lectern.
"Lei ha intenzione," proseguì l'altro, con l'atto minaccioso e iracondo di chi coglie un suo inferiore sull'intraprendere una ribalderia, "Lei ha intenzione di maritar domani Renzo Tramaglino e Lucia Modella!"	"And so you have it in mind," said the bravo in the threatening manner of a man who has caught a subordinate in the act of committing a blackguardly crime, "you have it in mind to marry Renzo Tramaglino and Lucia Mondella tomorrow!"

Source text	Target text
"Cioè . . ." rispose, con voce tremolante, don Abbondio: "cioè. Lor signori son uomini di mondo, e sanno benissimo come vanno queste faccende. Il povero curato non c'entra: fanno i loro pasticci tra loro, e poi . . ., e poi, vengon da noi, come s'andrebbe a un banco a riscotere: e noi . . ." noi siamo i servitori del comune."	"Well!" said Don Abbondio in a trembling voice, "well, you see . . . you gentlemen are men of the world, and realize how these things go. It's nothing to do with the poor curé; these people make their own muddled arrangements, and then . . . why, they come to us just as they might go to a bank to draw money . . . we are . . . just the servants of the community."
"Or bene," gli disse il bravo, all'orecchio, ma in tono solenne di comando, "questo matrimonio non s'ha da fare, nè domani, nè mai."	"Very well," said the bravo, speaking into the priest's ear, quietly, but in a tone of impressive command, "that wedding is not to take place. Not tomorrow, and not any other time either."

Comments

Time: there are various timeframes that affect this novel: it was published in the mid-nineteenth century; the story is set in the seventeenth century and is taken from near the beginning of the book; this translation is from 1972; these comments are made in 2019; the book has been read continuously in the original or in various translations since it was first published. The translator, Bruce Penman, remarks that previous translations (i.e., prior to 1972) are unconvincing in terms of language (some used "pseudo-archaic jargon") or have other failings, such as inaccuracies, or they were "extensively and badly cut." However, his translation could also be improved, as regards tone and emphasis.

1 *Register*: "Cosa comanda?" – Penman's version *What can I do for you?* conveys the sense but does not express the servility that Don Abbondio exhibits when confronted by two swashbuckling bravoes (such individuals had a reputation for abusive behaviour towards the local people). The use of "subito" (he responded *immediately*) also suggests he felt threatened. *What can I do for you?* is a rather banal phrase used in, for example, a customer service context. Here Don Abbondio's response is more along the lines of *How can I be of service, sir?*

2 *Language*: "Lei ha intenzione" is translated *And so you have it in mind*. The bravo wastes no time in delivering his curt message, which would suggest an equally curt rendering in the TL, such as *You intend*. Given that the phrase is repeated, then completed, it may be appropriate to provide a brusque rendering, which would emphasise the anger the bravo shows ("iracondo").

3   *Tone/emphasis*: "Sanno benissimo come vanno queste faccende" is trans-
     lated: *[you] realise how these things go*. Don Abbondio seems to be shrugging
     his shoulders, as he delivers this phrase and saying *You know only too well
     how these things go*.

4   *Tone*: "Il povero curato non c'entra: fanno i loro pasticci tra loro" is translated *it's
     nothing to do with the poor curé; these people make their own muddled arrange-
     ments*. Don Abbondio attempts to deflect any criticism of his actions by adopting
     a servile and piteous attitude: the phrase *nothing to do with* does not render the
     sense clearly, which is *the poor curé is not to blame*, while "fanno i loro pasticci"
     is a general criticism of local people, and *arrangements* (even if they are *mud-
     dled*) misses the point, which is that *these people tend to make a mess of things*.

5   *Emphasis*: "Questo matrimonio non s'ha da fare" is a very famous phrase, of
     great importance to the plot and often quoted; the translation *that wedding is
     not to take place. Not tomorrow, and not any other time either* while adequate,
     is slightly clumsy and not as forceful as the Italian, which could simply be ren-
     dered: *this marriage is not to take place. Not tomorrow. Never*. The paraphrase
     used by the translator to relay the sense of "mai" (*never*) weakens the empha-
     sis of the absolute form.

COMPARISON 3: English into German and Italian from *Harry Potter and the
Philosopher's Stone*, paperback edition, by J. K. Rowling, 1997, Bloomsbury Publishing Plc, London: 42–3.

Translation details

German version: *Harry Potter und der Stein des Weisen*, Carlsen Verlag
   GmbH, Hamburg (1998: 59), translated by Klaus Fritz.
Italian version: *Harry Potter e la pietra filosofale*, Salani Editore (1998: 52)
   translated by Marina Astrologo.

*The following passage appears in an early chapter of the first of J. K. Rowling's
Harry Potter books. Hagrid has located Harry at the home of the ghastly Dursley
family. Harry is astonished to find that he is a wizard and that he has been offered a
place at Hogwarts School of Witchcraft and Wizardry. Hagrid shows Harry a letter
confirming the place.*

Source Text (the text appears in italics in the English original)

HOGWARTS SCHOOL OF WITCHCRAFT AND WIZARDRY

*Headmaster: Albus Dumbledore
(Order of Merlin, First Class, Grand Sorc., Chf. Warlock,
Supreme Mugwump, International Confed. of Wizards)*

Dear Mr Potter,

We are pleased to inform you that you have a place at Hogwarts School of Witch-craft and Wizardry. Please find enclosed a list of all necessary books and equipment. Term begins on 1 September. We await your owl by no later than 31 July.

Yours sincerely,

Minerva McGonagall
Deputy Headmistress

Translation challenges

As the English text is being compared with two foreign versions, it may be useful to point out common features and challenges faced by the translators. Given that this was the first book in the series, the translators had no precedent; thus, the decisions they took could not be influenced by previous translations. Generally speaking, the translations follow the source text closely, as one would expect for this **format**, and use appropriate style, register and lexis, but some choices are idiosyncratic.

1   *Format*: The official letter format needs to have the same layout as the English. Not a problem technically speaking, but it also needs to achieve an equivalent effect on the target readerships.
2   *Abbreviations*: These add to the comical effect of the combination of formal writing and the "surreal" context. Again, it is about creating an equivalent effect but one which emphasises the comic aspect.
3   *Style and register*: The insertion of a formal letter in what is otherwise a highly colloquial context shows a humorous intent, which is intensified by Harry's perception of the obscure reference to "await your owl" with the reply and which creates a comic effect. It is not the actual words that are challenging but rather the context in which they arise.
4   *Lexis*: The main challenges are represented by the "magical" vocabulary, abbre-viated forms, proper nouns and neologisms.

German translation

HOGWARTS-SCHULE FÜR HEXEREI UND ZAUBEREI

Schulleiter: Albus Dumbledore
(Orden der Merlin, Erster Klasse, Großz., Hexenmst.
Ganz hohes Tier, Internationale Vereinig. d. Zauberer)

Sehr Geehrter Mr. Potter,
wir freuen uns, Ihnen mitteilen zu können, dass Sie an der Hogwarts-Schule für Hexerei und Zauberei aufgenommen sind. Beigelegt finden Sie eine Liste aller benötigen Bücher und Ausrüstungsgegenstände.

Das Schuljahr beginnt am 1. September. Wir erwarten Ihre Eule spätestens am 31 Juli.

Mit freundlichen Grüßen

Minerva McGonagall
Stellvertretende Schulleiterin

Comments

In terms of format, the German text replicates the English almost exactly, although the letter does not appear in italics. In style, official writing in German is (or sounds) as remote from the informal context as it does in English; therefore, the German mirrors the English effectively in reflecting authorial intention.

The abbreviations work well, possibly apart from *Großz*.

"Supreme Mugwump": the juxtaposition of the official-sounding "Supreme" with the curious compound "Mugwump" creates a humorous effect. The German *Ganz hohes Tier* (literally "very high animal" but more often used colloquially to mean a "big shot") does reflect the original meaning of the word, which derives from the Algonquian term for "great chief," and which was in use from the mid-nineteenth century. It is generally seen as a humorous term for a VIP, leader or boss. However, in the United States, for political and historical reasons, it came to embody the meaning of someone aloof from politics (politically disinterested). Clearly, in this context, the original meaning is intended, and the German solution sits well in context, particularly due to the juxtaposition between formal and informal discourse.

Italian translation

SCUOLA DI MAGIA E STREGONERIA DI HOGWARTS

Direttore: Albus Silente
(Ordine di Merlino, Prima Classe, Grande Esorcista, Stregone Capo,
Supremo Pezzo Grosso, Confed. Internaz. dei Maghi)

Caro Signor Potter,
Siamo lieti di informarLa che Lei ha diritto a frequentare la Scuola di Magia e Stregoneria di Hogwarts. Qui accluso troverà l'elenco di tutti i libri di testo e delle attrezzature necessarie.
I corsi avranno inizio il 1° settembre. Restiamo in attesa della Sua risposta via gufo entro e non oltre il 31 luglio p. v.

Con ossequi,

Minerva McGranitt
Vicedirettrice

Comments

The Italian format generally follows the English, with minor differences. The italics are retained. The style and register also reflect the English, in the use of formal letter-writing. The addition of *p.v.* to the date (i.e., *prossimo venturo*, meaning "of the current year" in context) accentuates the formality of the letter and contrasts with the unexpected *gufo* reference. Abbreviations are only used for the final element of the list of titles, possibly because the translator feared incomprehension if various abbreviated forms were adopted. Lexical use is more idiosyncratic than in the German version, as names are not transposed directly (with the exception of *Potter*). There is no apparent reason why "Albus Dumbledore" should be translated as *Albus Silente* (there is no causal link between Dumbledore and silent, though the alliteration of the "d" in Dumbledore may have induced the translator to attempt alliteration using "s"). "Minerva McGonagall" also undergoes a transformation: *Minerva McGranitt*, where *Granitt* has resonance with the stone granito/granite), in a possible (stereotypical) allusion to her (apparently) austere character. One rendering that works well, though, is *Supremo Pezzo Grosso* for "Supreme Mugwump," which contains the same juxtaposition for comic effect as in the English text of **formality**/informality.

COMPARISON 4: English into German and Spanish from *Harry Potter and the Chamber of Secrets*, by J. K. Rowling (first published 1998); this edition 2014, Bloomsbury Publishing Plc, London: 128.

Translation details

German version: *Harry Potter und die Kammer des Schreckens*, Carlsen Verlag GmbH, Hamburg (1999: 128) translated by Klaus Fritz.
Spanish version: *Harry Potter y la cámara secreta*, Ediciones Salmandra (1999: 120) translated by Adolfo Muñoz García and Nieves Martín Azofra.

The passage is taken from the beginning of Chapter 8, "The Deathday Party." Harry Potter is having a rather difficult time at Hogwarts School and the weather is not helping matters.

Source text

October arrived, spreading a damp chill over the grounds and into the castle. Madam Pomfrey, the nurse, was kept busy by a sudden spate of colds among the staff and students. Her Pepperup potion worked instantly, though it left the drinker smoking at the ears for several hours afterward. Ginny Weasley, who had been looking pale, was bullied into taking some by Percy. The steam pouring from under her vivid hair gave the impression that her whole head was on fire.

Raindrops the size of bullets thundered on the castle windows for days on end; the lake rose, the flower beds turned into muddy streams, and Hagrid's pumpkins swelled to the size of garden sheds. Oliver Wood's enthusiasm for regular training sessions, however, was not dampened, which was why Harry was to be found, late one stormy Saturday afternoon a few days before Halloween, returning to Gryffindor Tower, drenched to the skin and splattered with mud.

Translation challenges

There are no major challenges in the first paragraph, possibly with the exception of "her Pepperup potion," although some structural changes were made (in German), presumably to give a clearer and more logical organisation of the action and the impressions.

German translation

Es wurde Oktober und feuchte Kühle breitete sich über die Ländereien und das Schloss aus. Eine Jähe Erkältungswelle unter den Lehrern und Schülern hielt Madam Pomfrey, die Krankenschwester, in Atem. Ihr Aufpäppel-Trank wirkte zwar sofort, aber wer ihn getrunken hatte, dem rauchten danach noch stundenlang die Ohren. Percy Weasley drängte die etwas kränklich aussehende Ginny, ein paar Schlucke zu trinken, und sofort zischte Dampf unter ihrem feuerroten Haar hervor und es sah aus, als stünde ihr Kopf in Flammen.

Regentropfen, gross wie Gewehrkugeln, trommelten tagelang gegen die Schlossfenster; der See schwoll an, die Blumenbeete verwandelten sich in Schlammströme und Hagrids Kürbisse quollen zur Grösse von Gartenschuppen auf. Oliver Wood freilich liess sich nicht beirren und feuerte sie begeistert zu regelmässigem Training an. So befand sich Harry eines stürmischen Samstagsnachmittags bis auf die Haut durchweicht und schlammbespritzt auf dem Heimweg zum Turm des Gryffindors.

Comments

As mentioned, a particular lexical challenge is posed by "Pepperup," presumably an invented brand name for a tonic, rendered in the German by *Aufpäppel-Trank*. This made-up name works well in two ways: the verb *aufpäppeln* means to nurse someone back to health (by feeding them up), and the alliteration of the "p" directly evokes the idea of pepping someone up. The sentence containing the phrase "was bullied into taking some by Percy" obviously suggested a change of structure in German, from the passive into the active, with Percy (Ginny's brother) as the subject, rather than the agent. Here, the German verb *drängte* has slightly less force than "bullied" because it often has the sense of "urged." The English structure is complicated for translation purposes by the embedded relative clause ("who had been looking pale"). The German translator then combines the drastic (and comic) effect of the tonic with two conjunctions (*und*) and main clauses. Whether or not this works as well as the English is a moot point. The rather matter-of-fact sentence sequences in English play down the vivid effect, while accentuating the comic aspect. In the second paragraph, the description works well, although it is odd that the reference to "Halloween" is omitted, and it is unclear whether this was deliberate or unintentional.

Spanish translation

Llegó octubre y un frío húmedo se extendió por los campos y penetró en el castillo. La señora Pomfrey, la enfermera, estaba atareadísima debido a una repentina epidemia de catarro entre profesores y alumnos. Su poción Pepperup tenía efectos instantáneos, aunque dejaba al que la tomaba echando humo por las orejas durante varias horas. Como Ginny Weasley tenía mal aspecto, Percy le insistió hasta que la probó. El vapor que le salía de debajo del pelo producía la impresión de que toda su cabeza estaba ardiendo.

Gotas de lluvia del tamaño de balas repicaron contra las ventanas del castillo durante días y días; el nivel del lago subió, los arriates de flores se transformaron en arroyos de agua sucia y las calabazas de Hagrid adquirieron el tamaño de cobertizos. El entusiasmo de Oliver Wood, sin embargo, no se enfrió, y por este motivo Harry, a última hora de una tormentosa tarde de sábado, cuando faltaban pocos días para Halloween, se encontraba volviendo a la torre de Gryffindor, calado hasta los huesos y salpicado de barro.

Comments

Pepperup is retained in Spanish, without any attempt to create a neologism or pun. The reference to "pep up" would be lost on the target readers, unless they knew English well. The matter-of-fact organisation and lexical choice of the tonic's effect on Ginny creates a similar effect in Spanish, though not so effectively and comically as in English. In the second sentence of the second paragraph, the Spanish follows a pattern of phrase sequencing regulated by no less than six commas, making this a long and fragmented sentence. The decision in German to restructure and recalibrate seems more logical, in terms of organisation and flow control.

Pause for thought: If your language combination is English into German, Italian or Spanish, try your hand at translating the English text; then compare your version with the published one/s commented on here. If you do not offer any of these language combinations, write a couple of paragraphs of your own in English (or in your mother tongue) as a creative exercise, imagining a scene at Hogwarts at Halloween, and then identify potential translation challenges and strategies.

PART 4: EDITING TRANSLATIONS: A FEW TIPS

Translators are sometimes asked to edit work produced by non-native speakers of their first language. This often has to be done within a very short timescale and you may be paid at an hourly rate, which means that only essential changes can be incorporated. Apart from correcting spelling, grammar and punctuation, the editor needs to look at the **collocations** used. In an editing project involving the English version of a Russian academic website, the collocation "*education information resources*" was changed to "*education-related information resources*," for example, and "*a profound list of references*" was changed to "*an extensive list of references*."

When editing texts translated from Slavonic languages and others that do not have definite or indefinite articles, you will need to check whether the translator has put in articles where necessary. One module description for the previously mentioned website omitted the indefinite article when it said, "On successful completion of this module, students will be able to work *in team* and organize cooperation." You also need to ensure that articles such as *a* or *the* are not used where they are *not* required in the target language.

It is also important to check that "*and*" is inserted (*with or without an Oxford comma*) between the last two items in a list because the convention in some languages, such as Russian and French, is to use a comma here without the equivalent final *and*. So when editing, you need to correct "research, communication, social skills," for example, to "research, communication, *and* social skills"). Likewise, in many source languages, dashes are used to include additional information in parentheses, whereas English generally prefers commas. (See Pattison, A. and Sigareva N. *The Herzen Human Technology editing project. Modern concepts of university education.* St. Petersburg: Herzen University, 2009.)

For issues such as Oxford commas, translators working into English will find it advisable to consult a style guide. The publisher will sometimes supply their own guide to preferred usage, but if they don't, there are various style guides available online, including that used by the *Guardian* and the *Observer*, which can be found at www.theguardian.com/guardian-observer-style-guide. Another excellent style guide is available online on the University of Oxford's website: www.ox.ac.uk/sites/files/oxford/media_wysiwyg/University%20of%20Oxford%20Style%20Guide.pdf. Other useful resources include *The Sense of Style* by Stephen Pinker (2014) London: Penguin Books; *For Who the Bell Tolls* by David Marsh (2013) London: Guardian Books; *Eats, Shoots and Leaves* by Lynne Truss (2003) London: Profile Books; and the US classic *The Elements of Style* by William Strunk, Jr., originally published by Harcourt in New York in 1918. Similar style guides are available for French, German, Italian and Spanish.

When editing and revising, it is worth looking at the **register**, that is, at the level of language used. If the context is formal or scientific, you would usually expect to see the word *fungi* rather than *mushrooms* and in an academic text, *observations* instead of *comments*. You would not expect to see contracted forms, such as "*isn't*" or "*can't*" or slang words, such as *hype*, in a government report or in a piece of academic writing. Similarly, the word "*besides*" is more likely to be found in a novel than the more formal *moreover*.

When you're editing something, where do you stop?

Reading work out loud is the best way to decide where commas are really needed, and you won't go too far wrong if you add a comma where you need to stop to take a breath.

At the end of the day, the key issue is "acceptability." In other words, if the information content is clear and the message comes across without any glaring errors in syntax, spelling or grammar, the job is virtually done. All that is left for the editor or reviser to do is to check the house style. It is often worth making a note of each client's or publisher's preferences – they may vary. Some clients may insist on expressions such as "data is," rather than "data are," which is traditionally considered more grammatically correct since *data* is the plural form of the Latin noun *datum*.

Another thing to remember is that editing should be consistent: if you decide to change "techniques" to "strategies," for example, you need to sustain this through-out the text.

A further area where stylistic errors often creep into an English translation is when a gerund is used rather than a relative clause. An example of this can be found in the following translation, produced by Russian academics. Can you spot it? The edited version, which was entitled "The Modern Crisis: An Overview of the Philosophy of Culture," appeared in *The Anglo-Saxon Zugzwang: The Irrational Paradox of the Enlightenment*, a book by Nadezda Golik and Arkady Izvekov, which explores the effects of the Enlightenment on international philosophy and civiliza-tion (2017, St Petersburg: Altheia).

Here is the original English translation:

The culture of a society is an indicator of its *quality* and ability to make *order out of chaos*. The dynamics of cultural transformation: development, improve-ment, stagnation or a crisis. . . . The latter is generally understood as transition from one stage to another. The theory of a cultural crisis appeared first at the turn of the 20th century, with the word *crisis* occurring in more and more works. There were also other, even more sinister definitions, such as *down-fall*, *death* and *catastrophe*. Many scholars thought that man had not become happier from the successes of civilization, which is opposite to culture. Such thoughts were expressed in essays on philosophy, sociology, history, literature and art as well as memoirs of scientists, politicians and public leaders. The stratum of self-reflection in European culture is vast, and in its entirety clearly indicated the awareness of the symptoms of the crisis.

According to K. Mannheim, the mechanism of transformation of modern culture is related to the forms of dictatorship replacing *free forms*, "when mass democratic society is left alone". In the non-economic, cultural sphere there are the same processes under way. The parallel is not accidental: culture, as well as economy is a production sphere; it generates cultural values, "with the only difference in the scale of the processes".

The preceding translation was edited, very quickly, by an English translator. Can you analyse why the changes that are underlined in the following version were necessary? Would you have made additional or different changes? The original Russian text can be found in the Appendix.

The culture of a society is an indicator of its *quality* and <u>its</u> ability to make *order out of chaos*. The dynamics of cultural transformation <u>are</u> development, improvement, stagnation <u>or crisis</u>. . . . The latter is generally understood as transition from one stage to another. The theory of a cultural crisis <u>first appeared</u> at the turn of the 20th century, with the word *crisis* occurring in more and more works. There were also other, even more sinister definitions, such as *downfall*, *death* and *catastrophe*. Many scholars thought that <u>Man</u> had not become happier as a result of the successes of civilization, which <u>is the opposite of</u> culture. Such thoughts were expressed in essays on philosophy, sociology, history, literature and art <u>and also in</u> the memoirs of scientists, politicians and public leaders. The <u>level</u> of self-reflection in European culture is <u>vast and</u> in its entirety clearly <u>indicates an</u> awareness of the symptoms of the crisis.

According <u>to the sociologist</u> *Karl* Mannheim, the mechanism of transformation of modern culture is related to the forms of dictatorship <u>that replace</u> *free forms*, "when mass democratic society is left alone". In the non-economic, cultural sphere the same processes are under way. The parallel is not accidental: culture, as well as <u>the</u> economy is a production sphere; it generates cultural values, "with the only difference <u>being</u> in the scale of the processes."

Translation-editing and sub-editing exercise

Now it's your turn!

I. A further extract from a draft translation of *The Anglo-Saxon Zugzwang: The Irrational Paradox of the Enlightenment* is set out in the following. The task falls into two stages.

1   Correct the punctuation and grammar and adjust the style so that the target text could be considered professionally usable. These are changes that a *reviser* would be expected to make.

2   Rephrase or rewrite the text to render it more accessible to the average student of political science. These are the kinds of changes that the *editor* of a political textbook might wish to make if sufficient time were available.

Pause for thought: How much **revision** of the following draft translation could be considered as falling within the remit of a translator? *These are the only changes you could make in Stage 1 of the task.*

Are there any changes you would like to add to make the argument clearer? Do you think it would be justifiable for a translator to make these changes? The changes you make in Stage 2 of the task are those that **an editor** might decide to make. Most translators would regard such changes as being beyond their brief unless they had been expressly asked by the client to **edit** the text. Unauthorised editing constitutes **translator intrusion**, that is, unwarranted interference on the part of the translator.

Draft translation

Here is the text for you to revise/edit

Despite the shortsightedness of the powerful ones of this world both the revolution and its consequences are becoming universal: a new type of an individual is also emerging in numerous cultures. Both in the West and in the East there are obvious signs of a new individual – intellectually free and responsible for his freedom, which the realities of 21st century clearly demonstrate. *Democracy*, if mentioned at all, is of secondary relevance. The existential freedom and the political one are far from being the same. A freely emerged personality meaning and interaction-favoring formal rules do not overlap. Besides, one can be intellectually free being politically dependent – and vice versa. Therefore the consequences of the existential revolution may only be supplemented by the modern-day interpretation of democratic principles.

You will find specimen answers to this translation-editing task in the Appendix, after the Russian texts.

II. Now look at the following English text, taken from a (draft) translation of an article which appeared in *Le Figaro* (www.lefigaro.fr/culture/encheres/2019/01/10/03016-20190110ARTFIG00267-apres-trente-ans-d-absence-retour-triomphal-de-georges-mathieu-a-new-york.php) about an artist. You can either a) improve the English without any reference to the French text or b) edit the TT using the ST. Decide which words or phrases you think need changing, remembering that editing a text is not about rewriting it, and then edit the text to make it read fluently in English. (This task is also suitable for non-native speakers of English.)

TT

> Long time underrated, the French star of the 1950–1970s takes his revenge. A flagship exhibition to restore his rating has been missing in the United States. The market has been waiting for nearly thirty years for a masterful exhibition. After a long purgatory, his work is starting to interest the market again. It also marks the beginning of a readjustment of his unjustified low rating to give his prices a boost internationally.

ST

> Longtemps sous-cotée, la star française des années 1950–1970 prend sa revanche. Il lui manquait une exposition phare aux États-Unis pour redorer sa cote. . . . Le marché attendait depuis bientôt trente ans une exposition magistrale aux États-Unis. . . . Après un long purgatoire, il commence à nouveau à intéresser le marché. Cela marque aussi le début d'un réajustement de sa cote anormalement basse, en lui donnant un sacré coup de boost, avec des prix à l'échelle internationale.

III. The following text is an excerpt from a factsheet handed out by a hotel in Florence to foreign visitors. Highlight what you feel are incorrect or inappropriate words or expressions; then produce a polished, edited version of the text in English. (If you wish to edit the translation with reference to the Italian text, see Appendix, p. 130 for the source text.)

Palace's history

> The Gianfigliazzai Palace, on the Lungarno Corsini, constituted the most important nucleus of the numerous houses belonged to the homonym family up to the end of 1700. On the elegant building crowned by an ample loggia, from 1427 during the centuries numerous restructurings were performed. In 1818 with the extinction of the Gianfigliazzi, the building was destined to hotel with the name "Delle Quattro Stagioni." Illustrious personalities stayed here, among them the poet Alexander Manzoni which referring to the Arno river wrote the famous sentence "in its waters I rinsed my rags." The Palace also hosted for long periods Luigi Bonaparte King of Holland who became its owner in 1828. Here was born and lived for many years Virginia, the Countess of Castiglione, known for her charm as well as for her friendship with Napoleon III of France. . . .
>
> Known for both the beautiful interiors and the pompous receptions, Palazzo Gianfigliazzi became one of the brightest and exclusive "salotti" in the city, quoted by Hippolite Taine in his "Voyage en Italie," as "the decoration of Florence."

Pause for thought: What skills have you acquired or developed from editing the preceding passages? If you are not a native speaker of English, how confident would you be about taking on an editing task in English? Bearing in mind that editing timeframes are usually very short, in a professional context, what time is there for research (on cultural references and so on)?

This chapter has shown how translators navigate the choppy waters of translating literary and semi-literary texts, the many types of challenges they face and some of the strategies they adopt to tackle these challenges. It has also shown that there is unlikely to be a translation that satisfies every critic, linguist or reader, whether this is due to the relationship with the source text or the target language. Last but not least, it has shown that there is clearly a need for a creative approach to resolving such challenges, albeit within the constraints of the source text.

The next chapter aims to help you improve your target language skills and the general quality of your translations.

CHAPTER 4

How to enhance your writing skills

In Chapters 2 and 3, we introduced you to analytical (or "deconstructive") methods of preparing a text for translation and to criteria for evaluating existing translations. Chapter 3 presented worked examples that analysed four English texts; annotated translations of four texts translated from English into French, German, Italian and Spanish; annotated translations of four texts translated from French, German, Italian and Spanish into English; translation comparisons; and hints on editing translations.

In the present chapter, however, we will turn our attention to preparing *you*, a translator and "writer by proxy," to tackle literary-type texts and initiating you into creative and constructive methods of improving the quality of your translations. We have also included some "workouts with words" to help you extend your active vocabulary, either in English or in your own target language.

One key facility that translators and writers have in common is the ability to work wonders with words. This was more widely acknowledged in the second half of the twentieth century, which saw publishers giving more credit to translators and the emergence of the translator/writer and translator/poet. Well-known figures in this category include the playwright and novelist Michael Frayn, the Mexican Nobel Prize-winner Octavio Paz, the Irish poet Seamus Heaney and the British poet and critic Michael Hamburger. Michael Frayn translated Anton Chekhov's plays from the Russian; Octavio Paz, who had lived in a few countries during his career as a Mexican diplomat, translated from several languages, including Chinese, English, French, Japanese, Portuguese, Sanskrit and Swedish. Seamus Heaney's remaking of the Old English epic poem *Beowulf* won the Whitbread Book of the Year Award in 2000, and he received considerable posthumous acclaim when his complete translation of Virgil's *Aeneid* Book VI was published in 2016. Michael Hamburger, for his part, made a plethora of German poets accessible to English readers through his translations of Benn, Celan, Enzensberger, Hölderlin, Sebald and others.

For translation students and for translators who do not usually work with literary-type material, creative writing is an effective and enjoyable way to add new tools to your toolbox and become even better at crafting a text. In this section, we will introduce you to some of the stylistic and linguistic "tricks" that writers use to hook their readers, demonstrating how a piece of writing is generated and encouraging you to get under the writer's skin and even to think like a writer rather than as a translator.

Because we believe that this book and this chapter in particular could be useful to students of world literature and of English language or creative writing, this chapter has a wider focus. It includes various writing tasks, many of which were devised for use in multilingual *Painting with Words* workshops for translators and in more general writers' workshops. It is up to you, the reader, to decide which tasks you wish to tackle in order to enhance your writing skills.

FINDING YOUR VOICE AND CAPTURING OTHER VOICES

Professional singers may often have a wide repertoire spanning several musical genres, yet those who become household names, like Edith Piaf, tend to have a very distinctive voice. The same applies to many successful writers – their voice is original enough to have attracted a publisher's interest. One secret of successful translation is the knack of capturing an author's voice. Before you can do this to the best of your ability, you need to find your own writer's voice.

The following writing exercises should stimulate your creativity and help you to explore your own voice. Once you have found it, you will be better able to appreciate those features of another writer's voice that make it special and different from everyone else's, which is particularly important when translating literary-type texts. It is possible to appreciate an author's voice *intellectually* by analysing and "deconstructing" his or her work, but it is only when you can understand it at an *emotional* level that you will be able to do full justice to an author whose work you are translating, without of course allowing your own voice to intrude on the author's. If we take an example from a different area of creative endeavour, art students often visit art galleries during their studies. With the help of their tutor, they can gain an academic insight into the techniques and strategies the artist used, but as they become more advanced practitioners of their craft, they are encouraged to try to copy or "transcribe" one of the great masters. This hands-on and more emotional experience of the act of creation, even if it is by proxy, helps them to determine which, if any, of the artist's strategies will work for them as they start to develop their own style and produce original work.

The aim of our writing tasks is to give you the chance to create your own source texts and, in the case of bilingual or multilingual groups of students, to allow you the opportunity to be translated. This is the chance for you to defy the fictitious mathematician created by the early eighteenth-century writer Baron Charles de Montesquieu, who was somewhat disparaging about translation. His mathematician told another character, a translator, that if he carried on translating forever, nobody would ever translate him! (*Lettres persanes* [*Persian Letters*], 1721: letter 128). You and your colleagues or classmates can prove him wrong if you each produce an original piece of writing and ask a translator working in the opposite direction of the same language pair to translate it for you.

The greater facility with language that you will acquire by experiencing the thrills of painting pictures with words will not only give you a glimpse into the secrets of the craft, it will also help you to become a more instinctive translator, more aware of the choices an author must make and more able to account for them in your target texts.

In these tasks, you will probably find it easier to write in your first language or in the one you dream in most. In a foreign language class or workshop, however, the exercise can be carried out in the language the students are studying.

Try to be spontaneous, drawing on a more primal level of consciousness, and if possible, carry on writing until you have put all your ideas down. You can check the spelling and grammar later.

WHERE DO YOU START AND HOW CAN YOU FIND INSPIRATION?

Writers draw their ideas from memories, both their own and other people's, from paintings and photographs, from conversations they have overheard, from historical documents or simply from daydreams. When you are daydreaming, you may find yourself wondering, "What would happen if . . .?" This question can lead to the creation of an entire world.

To get you started, we have devised an exercise that links up with our key themes of time, context and culture and will also give you an insight into their role in weaving the fabric of a fictitious world. This exercise has been used in creative writing seminars for translators and works well in foreign language classes too as a language enhancement exercise. Because most modern fiction tends to be character-driven, the task involves creating a character. You will also need to select a setting in a specific time and culture.

When you tackle the task, you will probably need to answer some of the five questions that journalists refer to as the five Ws (Who? What? Why? Where? When?). Traditionally, before the days of desktop publishing, these questions had to be answered in the report's first paragraph or so because newspaper articles had to be cut from the bottom up if the production editor ran out of space to fit in the whole text.

Such an assignment fits well into a classroom context because people can bounce ideas off each other, stimulating a kind of collective creativity. It also works for individual private study but is more fun if you can ask a friend or family member to help you.

> **Task 1: Creating a character and a setting (an individual or group exercise)**
>
> Draw the rough outline of a person in felt-tip pen on a large sheet of paper (A3 or bigger if possible – last year's calendar is fine for this task).
>
> a) To begin with, focus on the *who* and the *what*. Fill in the outline you have drawn with details of the following: their birthday, age, birth-sign, what they usually had for breakfast, what language they spoke, whom or what they loved/hated, their greatest fear, what newspaper they read, their aim in life and what made them special.
> b) Try to decide *where* and *when* they live/lived. Once you have done this, give them a name. The name needs to match the time and the culture and the character's social position.

If there are children in your extended family, you can use your character as the basis of a story written especially for them. To flesh out fictional characters, a writer needs to explore why people act in a particular way. The *time* in which you set the action may have created an obstacle to overcome. Someone living one hundred years ago or in a different culture is likely to have encountered or to encounter context-driven problems that differ from those we are familiar with nowadays or in the West. They might have struggled to get a job so that they could afford to get married (a problem that still prevails in present-day India, for example) or could have found it hard to break through the barriers of class, gender or circumstances of birth (such as the stigma of illegitimacy).

When deciding on the *context* and a *cultural settin*g for your story, you will find it helps if you tap into your own memories of staying with grandparents and elderly relatives when you were small. What did their house smell of? What sounds did you hear? What shadows were cast on the wall as you tried to drop off to sleep?

EXPLORING A THEME

The next question you need to consider still addresses the issue of *what*, but it focuses on the whole picture, rather than on details, so that it can become clear in your own mind what the main theme of your writing is. Defining your theme will help to improve your thinking skills and develop your understanding of the power of words. An effective way to do this is to imagine that a friend asks you, "What is your story about?" Try to tell him or her in thirty words or less. If you can do that, you are well on the way towards writing a logline. We discussed the concept briefly in Chapter 2, but now we will be encouraging you to try to craft a logline of your own. You can find examples of successful loglines for filmscript ideas that later became box office hits at www.filmdaily.tv/logline/top-box-office-logline-examples.

Here are three of them to give you an idea of the basic principles:

The aging patriarch of an organized crime dynasty transfers control of his clandestine empire to his reluctant son.

(The Godfather)

Set in unoccupied Africa during the early days of World War II: An American expatriate meets a former lover, with unforeseen complications.

(Casablanca)

Two imprisoned men bond over a number of years, finding solace and eventual redemption through acts of common decency.

(The Shawshank Redemption)

Although loglines are usually confined to the film industry, they are a very good exercise for writers and translators because they help you to master the art of encapsulating the emotional appeal of a story in one sentence. This is a useful skill when it comes to pitching a proposal to a publisher for a new book translation or writing project.

Here's a logline that sums up the plot of Patrick Rotman's *Un homme à histoires*, extracts of which were included in Chapter 3:

As France loses its hold in Indochina and trouble brews in North Africa, a future President schemes his way into political office and starts a secret second family.

The following example tells the story of Ann Pattison's play for radio *New Zealand Rose*, which is based on a true story. An extract from this was published in *Writing on Glass* (2018: Caper Press, London). The logline reads

A seven-year-old girl from a children's home has to leave New Zealand to live in Britain with wealthy relatives she has never met but her feckless mother doesn't turn up to say goodbye.

You will see from these examples that the ideas in loglines are usually expressed in generic, rather than specific terms and use active rather than passive verbs, as in much popular tabloid journalism. Traditionally, the scriptwriter has just one sentence in which to sell an idea.

Along similar lines, for an academic translation brief referred to on p. 54, the French author (Pierre-Jean Luizard) kindly supplied the English translator with a title in English, which summed up the content of his article in a dozen words: *Damascus and Cairo: two heads of Hussein for two kinds of worship*. Like a logline, this title provided the translator with very useful contextual information indicating that the text would be dealing with two conflicting cultural traditions.

Now it's your turn. If you have ever had to produce an abstract or a précis for a client or academic supervisor, the analytical skills you applied to that process will be useful for this task. Or if you have translated marketing or publicity material, an awareness of how copywriters promote a product will help you with the more creative aspects of drafting a logline.

Task 2: Writing a logline

Choose a novel or play that you might like to translate one day, or think of a story of your own that you would like to tell.

Once you know the main character, write a logline to pitch your proposal to a publisher. Remember, you have one sentence in which to sell the story.

Use active rather than passive verbs.

Show who this person is, what they want and what stands in their way.

Let us assume that you now have a main character, a setting and a theme for your writing project. You have also considered the three perspectives of time, context and culture. At last, you are ready to add the third dimension and make your imagined universe spring into life.

INVOKING THE SENSES

To add this extra dimension, many writers draw you into their world by appealing to your senses. In his Booker Prize-winning novel about the Burma railroad *The Narrow Road to the Deep North* (2014: 1, London: Vintage Books), Richard Flanagan opens the book by invoking the sense of *sight*:

Why at the beginning of things is there always light? Dorrigo Evans' earliest memories were of sun flooding a church hall in which he sat with his mother and grandmother. A wooden church hall. Blinding light and him toddling back and forth, in and out of its transcendent welcome, into the arms of women.

As you read this, you find yourself blinking or reaching for your sunglasses.

Sound can likewise be used effectively if the lexis is carefully chosen to exploit figures of speech such as alliteration, assonance or onomatopoeia. A good example of how all these stylistic devices can be used to create vivid images appeared in Sebastian Barry's 2014 novel *The Temporary Gentleman*, in which he describes the aftermath of a torpedo hit:

> Everything roared for that moment, the high night sky of blankening stars, the great and immaculate silver serving dish of the sea itself, the rended ship, the offended and ruined men.

Here *roared* is an example of **onomatopoeia**, the *high night sky* features assonance with the repeated "i" sounds and *silver serving dish of the sea* is alliterative with its sequence of "s" sounds.

Poetry abounds in examples of alliteration and assonance. In "The Bees," the title poem of her first collection as poet laureate, Carol Ann Duffy opens with

> *Here are my bees,*
> *brazen, blurs on paper,*
> *besotted; buzzwords, dancing*
> *their flawless, airy maps.*

The first chapter of Kate Furnivall's novel *The Russian Concubine* (2007, New York: Berkley Books) uses all three of these figures of speech to convey the dramatic tensions of 1917 Russia. Can you spot them?

> The train growled to a halt. Grey steam belched from its heaving engine into the white sky, and the twenty-four freight carriages behind bucked and rattled as they lurched shrieking to a standstill.

This passage transports readers to another time and place because they *can hear* the train stopping suddenly.

In *The Hare with Amber Eyes*, Edmund de Waal's Costa 2010 prize-winning biographical account of the story of his family's collection of *netsuke* or Japanese miniature carvings, the author appeals to the reader's sense of *touch* when he explains what it feels like to take a beautiful object in his hand:

> And that opening glass door and the moment of looking, then choosing, and then reaching in and then picking up is a moment of seduction, an encounter between a hand and an object that is electric.
>
> (2010, London: Chatto & Windus)

In the opening paragraph of *Chocolat*, Joanne Harris describes how Vianne and her daughter arrive in a village on Shrove Tuesday. You can really *smell* these pancakes.

We came on the wind of the carnival. A warm wind for February, laden with the hot greasy scents of frying pancakes and sausages and powdery-sweet waffles cooked on the hotplate right there by the roadside.

(2000, London: Black Swan)

The most famous literary example of an appeal to the senses is, of course, Marcel Proust's use of *taste* with his *madeleine*, the little cake that suddenly brings memories of childhood flooding back to the hero of *A la Recherche du temps perdu*.

The next task will show you how sensual stimuli can help you to get started. If you want to improve on or add to what you wrote for Task 1, you should find the stimuli described in Task 3a particularly helpful. In writing workshops and combined bilingual writing/translating workshops, this activity has proved to be very popular and has inspired some excellent work. It has also led to stimulating discussions relating to cultural gaps where the translator pointed out the difficulty in choosing the correct equivalent term in the target language for words such as "*mémé*" the French affectionate term for a grandmother or the English term "insiders" (used in the context of a group of young people who frequented a particular café).

Scents and smells that work well for this task are spices such as cinnamon sticks, cloves or nutmeg; the zest of a lemon or orange; a sprig of lavender or rosemary; and carbolic or coal tar soap. When this task is used as a workshop activity, volunteers take it in turn to be blindfolded while someone exposes them to various smells and hands them different objects to feel, asking them to describe the thoughts and memories that these things trigger.

Task 3a): Writing in response to sensual stimuli

1   Choose an evocative piece of music and set it playing in the background. TV theme tunes, classical guitar music and film scores, especially from Westerns, are great for this.

Does the music take you back to a special place or time in your life or even transport you to a different culture? Describe this time and place.

2   Look in your kitchen cupboard and take out a few spices and then go into the bathroom and find a soap or shampoo with a specific scent. Do any of these smells or scents help to bring back memories of your childhood? Write down the first thoughts that come into your head.

You can use any *form* you like: poetry, prose, blank verse, a **shape poem**, or even a scene for a play. Do whatever comes most naturally to you.

A further literary example of how a writer invokes the senses to tell a story can be found in Patrick Süsskind's 1985 novel *Das Parfum* (published by Diogenes Verlag in Zurich). The main protagonist is an evil genius, whose activities, the narrator claims, are confined to one sphere of activity that leaves no trace in history, that of smells. We are told this on the very opening page, in which the expression *es stanken* is used three times to stress the general stink that pervaded French cities, particularly Paris, in the eighteenth century. Süsskind describes, for example, how the streets stank of dung, the backyards stank of urine and the stairwells stank of rotten wood and rat droppings. The verb *stinken* appears several more times on the next page and is applied even to the king and queen. In contrast, the wet nurse paid to feed the baby who was born under a stinking fish stall on a stifling hot day amid all the stench returns him to the local priest because he has no smell at all, which makes her feel very uncomfortable.

FEEDBACK ON TASK 3A)

Invoking the senses and making readers see and hear what someone is experiencing is a way of *showing* readers what is happening, instead of assuming the role of an **omniscient narrator** and *telling* them. In his environment-embracing novel *The Truth* (2012, London: Orion, pp. 90–91), Michael Palin very successfully speeds up the pace by making readers feel as if they are there with his main protagonist Mabbut:

> Then a sudden sharp cry from farther up the street cut through the ambient noise. Mabbut stood on tiptoe, craning his neck for a better view. A crowd was converging on a tilted autorickshaw. He could hear shouts, raised voices, people thumping the roof of the vehicle. He half walked, half ran to join the group of onlookers. Anger and argument filled the air as arms were raised and fists clenched.

When you read this passage, you feel as if you are watching and hearing the events unfold.

The preceding narrative is told in the past tense, but some writers achieve a sense of immediacy by writing in the present tense. Here is your chance to explore what works best for you. Often, a writer will include a prologue in the present tense and then revert to the past for the rest of the novel.

Task 3b): Changing the perspective

Did you write in the *past* tense?

Take a fresh page and rewrite your description in the *present* tense.

If you wrote in the *present*, rewrite your piece in the *past*.

If the passage you have written is set *in your own culture*, transpose it into a *different cultural and/or historical setting*.

Which version do you prefer?

VIEWPOINT

First person

In Chapter 2, we considered viewpoint from a translator's perspective. The writer, however, must consider different factors when deciding whose point of view to adopt when telling a story. The various viewpoints each have their advantages and drawbacks. For instance, by telling a story in the first person, a writer has the advantage of immediacy and soon captures the reader's interest. Although new writers were advised against adopting this point of view in the past, the technique works well in Gail Honeyman's highly successful début novel *Eleanor Oliphant Is Completely Fine* (2017, London: Harper Collins) because it helps to highlight Eleanor's loneliness. The same first-person point of view is likewise used in Patrick Rotman's *Un Homme à Histoires*.

However, the focus is restricted because everything is seen subjectively through the eyes of one person, who may be a reliable narrator but may also have a distorted view of events or misrepresent them. Some writers deliberately create an unreliable protagonist and let him or her tell the story because this is a way of adding an element of surprise. Readers are puzzled because nothing is quite as it seems, and they do not know whether they can believe what the narrator says or not. In Paula Hawkins' bestseller *The Girl on the Train* (2015, Hull: Riverhead Books), the first-person viewpoint character is an alcoholic, which helps to sustain the suspense. In Gail Honeyman's story, Eleanor Oliphant's account of events cannot be trusted because she has suffered traumatic experiences, which result in her unintentionally giving the reader misleading information. In crime fiction, however, it can be disconcerting when you have begun to identify with the narrator only to discover in the dénouement that you had put your trust into the hands of the murderer! Agatha Christie used this device on one occasion at least, but some readers may have felt cheated because an unspoken contract of trust had been broken.

In recent popular fiction, a common device is to use multiple viewpoints, with the first chapter told by one character in the first person and the next by another, also in the first person. This is a strategy adopted by Sebastian Faulks in *Paris Echo* (2018, London: Hutchinson), where readers receive alternate first-hand accounts of their experiences of Paris from Hannah, an American researcher writing about the imprint made by the German occupation on the lives of women who had lived in the city, and from Tariq, a young runaway from Morocco.

The third person viewpoint is more objective, giving the reader a clearer panoramic overview of events, but it is more remote. In Mitch Cullin's 2005 novel *Mr Holmes* (paperback edition: 2015, Canongate Books: Edinburgh), the narrative is told in a traditional third-person style, but this is interjected with first person extracts from a manuscript that Holmes was supposed to have been working on. To help the reader to negotiate the text, the line spacing is wider in these sections so that it is easier to see who is telling the story.

An omniscient (all-knowing) third-person narrator has an unlimited knowledge of everything that is going on, which nowadays is considered to be unrealistic because an observer is not usually present during private conversations and interactions, for instance. The US author and blogger K. M. Weiland makes a distinction between this **omniscient third person point of view (POV)**, the **distant third person** and the **deep third person** (www.helpingwritersbecomeauthors. com/third-person-pov/ last accessed on 1.02.2019). Weiland explains that, unlike an omniscient third person POV, the "distant third person" is confined to describing the action from one character's point of view at a time. The "deep third person" POV goes one step further and becomes almost an extension of the first person, taking readers right inside the narrator's head. This kind of narrator can only tell readers about his or her own thoughts and feelings. Other characters' actions are seen through the filter of the narrator's reaction to them or through what they heard the other person say.

An example of the deep third person can be found in the prologue that opens Kate Atkinson's novel *Transcription* (2018: 3, London: Doubleday):

"Miss Armstrong? MISS Armstrong, can you hear me?"

She could, although she didn't seem able to respond. She was badly damaged. Broken. She had been hit by a car. It might have been her own fault, she had been distracted.

Despite the use of the third person singular pronoun *she*, Miss Armstrong's response to the question reflects her thoughts and her reaction to the accident. The words *broken* and *distracted* seem unlikely to have been used by an objective observer and therefore take the reader straight into the character's head.

Once you have selected your viewpoint character, start to think about their *voice*. What would they sound like? The lexis employed here is of a fairly formal register, suggesting an older, well-educated protagonist. In contrast, a young woman talking excitedly to her friend on her phone from the train would use more informal language, as would a laconic teenager overheard on the bus. They might speak with a local accent or include the glottal stop after a "t" sound as South Londoners often do. Miss Armstrong's grammar is impeccable, but a character from a large housing estate might say "you was" instead of "you were."

Because she found the first person too limited in perspective and wanted to show another character's view of events, a colleague in a writing group who was revising the first draft of her novel decided she needed to change the viewpoint from first to deep third person throughout, which was a very daunting task! Even with a short piece, changing the viewpoint can be challenging, but it can lead to a startling improvement in reader engagement. When you work on the next part of Task 3, you will be experimenting with different viewpoints.

It is not only characters that have viewpoints: authors do too, particularly those of non-fiction works in the humanities and social sciences. This means that, as a translator, you will need to determine the author's viewpoint or stance. Authors are not always impartial: they may have a hidden agenda. You can often identify if they have taken a particular stance by looking out for statements that are based on assumptions, allusions or inferences. A failure to spot any bias can lead to misunderstandings or misconceptions, and there is often a need to bridge a gap between cultures or historical periods.

Pause for thought: Can you think of instances when you as a translator should reveal an author's hidden agenda?

Are there any scenarios where it would be acceptable for a translator to allow an author's personal agenda to remain concealed?

To create an authentic voice, you may find it helpful to consider the *register* that a character would use in various social contexts. Register (or level of language) plays an important role in any piece of writing and will reflect how subjective or objective the author's viewpoint is. Questions the translator needs to consider include whether the sentence structures and syntax are simple or complex and the tone the author has adopted. Is it impersonal, as in a formal report, or personal, as in an email to a friend?

Task 3c): Changing the viewpoint

In Task 3a), did you write in the first person or third person?

Rewrite your piece from a different viewpoint. See if you can bring out the character's voice.

SHOW; DON'T TELL

At the start of a novel, some writers *tell* you a character's previous life history, following the predilection for omniscient narrative that was prevalent in the nineteenth century. For example, in the first chapter of Michael Palin's *The Truth* (ibid), readers are told that

Gales had blown hard across the muddy bay this last week but had dropped quite suddenly overnight. . . . Last night the oil company had given a party.

The repeated use of the pluperfect tense with "had blown," "had dropped" tends to slow down the pace of the action, which is acceptable in a more descriptive passage such as this, but if it happens too often, the reader could lose interest in the story because the modern trend is to avoid too much "*telling*" and *show* the reader what is happening instead.

Task 4: Writing the "backstory"

In the preceding extract, can you think of other ways to fill in what is known as the "**backstory**"?

One trick you could use to hold the reader's interest is to have the character writing in his or her diary or sending an email or text to a friend.

What do you think Palin's hero might have said? Write an email or text from him to a friend, including the information set out in the short extract. You will find a specimen message at the end of this chapter.

Taking your readers inside a character's head is an example of how to *show*, rather than *tell*, them what is going on. Some writers use diary entries to tell a character's backstory, but in *A Legacy of Spies*, John Le Carré uses Secret Service reports and transcripts of taped interviews (2018: 121–122 and 169–172, Penguin Books). These have the advantage of added authenticity, yet the drawback is that the more impersonal style of such "official" documents can slow down the pace.

The next task is a word-building exercise to help you exploit your own word bank.

Task 5: Workout with words

Make a list of as many words as you can to describe the smells and sounds you experimented with in Task 3a). If you are stuck, use a thesaurus to help you. Then take a soft towel or a silk scarf and hold it against your skin or stroke your family pet. Run your hand along a rough wall or a piece of sandpaper. Jot down as many adjectives as you can to describe them.

Now think of the last time you were on a busy dockside or railway station.

Write down all the sounds you can remember hearing.

When you have finished, compare your lists with the suggestions given at the end of this chapter.

SUSPENSION OF DISBELIEF

Writers of fiction often use very explicit details to trick the reader into accepting an improbable or even impossible situation as if it were real. This is called "**suspension of disbelief**," which means, for instance, that if you asked teenagers to believe in the idea of a boy wizard, they would say, "Get real!" yet J. K. Rowling sold this concept to them by creating a boarding school that was in many respects like any other educational establishment, confidently describing all the teachers and the curriculum so meticulously that readers soon forgot that this was quite impossible. Providing authentic details such as the reference to "Platform nine and three-quarters" is a clever way to suspend disbelief and make the target reader accept an improbable or impossible premise.

Further examples of believable fantasy can be found in the **magical realism** genre popular in South American writing (e.g., Isabel Allende's 1982 novel *The House of the Spirits*) or in some French spin-offs that emulate this genre. For instance, Marc Levy's prize-winning first novel features a woman in a coma who is able to go back to her old flat and hide in a cupboard where the new tenant "finds" her and falls in love with her! (*"Et si c'était vrai…"* 2000, Paris: Robert Laffont). They have several incredible adventures culminating in his kidnapping her from the hospital ward and transporting her in a stolen ambulance to a house by the sea to stop the doctors from switching off her life support machine. The trick this author uses to suspend the reader's disbelief is increasing the pace by using short, snappy sentences with lots of dialogue. Everything moves so fast that there is hardly any time to stop and question what is happening. It seems strange, preposterous even, yet you are so keen to know whether his plan will work that you have to keep turning the page. Although written in French, the story is set in San Francisco, and the characters are American. Displacing the setting to a different *cultural context* is another factor that helps the writer to make a far-fetched premise appear more credible.

> **Pause for thought:** If you were to translate such a novel into your target language, how would you deal with the displacement between the source language culture (in the preceding case, French) and the context in which the novel is set (in this case, American)?

BREAKING THE MOULD

Many writers, artists and musicians recognise the need to be original, so they often try to be unconventional and surprise or even shock people. Claude Debussy said, "Works of art make rules; rules do not make works of art" (www.brainyquote.com/quotes/claude_debussy_204267).

An illustration of how effective it can be to defy convention can be found in the publicity posters that were once put up in a London high school to advertise a biology lecture. Since this was scheduled to take place just before Halloween, the posters bore the eye-catching title "Are you a zombie?" Local biologists, who were also invited, were informed in their professional journal that the topic was "Sodium Ion Transport"! Of course, the hall was full of students, attracted by the quirky title, with only a scattering of professional biologists.

When writers wish to break the mould, they often do so by identifying the reader's expectations and then either satisfying or partly satisfying them with a promise of something even better than what they had anticipated or throwing them completely off-balance by changing the direction of their thoughts. Another strategy they sometimes use is introducing an everyday object or situation but looking at it from an entirely new angle. The painter-poet Guillaume Apollinaire achieved this by creating his *Calligrammes* or shape poems, in which the words were arranged to form the shape of a familiar object or landmark, such as a bird, the head and front legs of a horse, a hand, and the Eiffel Tower.

> **Pause for thought:** Why do you think it is important for a translator to be aware that an author is "breaking the rules"? How would you account for this in your target text?
>
> How would you go about translating one of Apollinaire's shape poems into your target language?

Another way of breaking the rules is to adopt the linguistic strategy of using an unusual collocation, that is, an unexpected combination of words, such as nouns and verbs or nouns and adjectives; for example, the title of the 2001 film about John Forbes Nash, winner of the Nobel Prize for economics, juxtaposes the adjective *beautiful* with the unexpected noun *mind*. We expect to see a noun like *day* collocating with *beautiful*, and a more conventional adjective to describe a *mind* would be *brilliant*. This resulted in *A Beautiful Mind* being a title that was easy to remember because it made people sit up and think and wonder what to expect.

Such unusual collocations are frequently found in poetry and in the works of the Welsh poet Dylan Thomas in particular. The final line of this extract from the poem he wrote in memory of Ann Jones, "After the Funeral" (from *The Collected Poems of Dylan Thomas*, 1934–1952 [1953, rev. ed. 1956]), includes a typical example of Dylan Thomas's originality.

> *Her flesh was meek as milk, but this skyward statue*
> *With the wild breast and blessed and giant skull*
> *Is carved from her in a room with a wet window*
> *In a fiercely mourning house in a crooked year.*

A figure of speech that extends the concept inherent in original collocations is **oxymoron**, which usually involves not just an unusual juxtaposition of words but what may appear to be a contradiction in terms, such as "sweet sorrow" in Shakespeare's *Romeo and Juliet*. A French example of this figure of speech would be *un silence éloquent* (an eloquent silence), an even better example of which is the

Spanish phrase *silencio atronador* (thunderous silence). Other Spanish examples of oxymoron are *calma tensa* (tense calm) and *secreto a voces* (open secret).

If you are aware when an author is using unusual collocations, you can then try to ensure that your translation has an equivalent effect on the reader, that is, adopting the strategy of **dynamic equivalence** described by the Bible translation scholar Eugene Nida in 1982 in *The Theory and Practice of Translation* (1982, Leiden, Netherlands: Brill). See also p. 30.

HOOKS

Most of the examples quoted in this chapter come from authors with a fresh voice, which is what readers and publishers look for in new writing. Many writers seeking to be original enough to land a publishing contract try to devise a first sentence that will startle the reader. This is known as a "**hook**" (French *accroche*, Italian *gancio d'apertura*, German *narrativer Haken* and Spanish *gancho*). Franz Kafka's novella *Die Verwandlung* (*The Metamorphosis*, 1917, Leipzig, Kurt Wolff Verlag) begins with such a line:

> Als Gregor Samsa eines Morgens aus unruhigen Träumen erwachte, fand er sich in seinem Bett zu einem ungeheueren Ungeziefer verwandelt. (Muir translation: "As Gregor Samsa awoke one morning from uneasy dreams he found himself transformed in his bed into a gigantic insect.")

Not only does Kafka shock you with this horrifying opening, he also takes you straight into the action by beginning with a crisis in his protagonist's life, rather than leading you in gently with an introduction to Gregor's backstory. Starting at a time when everything changes is a popular technique in modern fiction.

The African-American Nobel Prize-winner Toni Morrison opened her ground-breaking book *Beloved*, the sensational and heart-breaking tale of a former slave, haunted by memories of her horrendous past and of her dead baby, with a reference to the *context* in which these events took place. The story begins with the house, No. 124, which is personified. "124 was spiteful. Full of a baby's venom." The next section likewise starts in a similar way "124 was loud" and the third with "124 was quiet" (Morrison, 1987, New York: Alfred A. Knopf). The repetition is an additional device that serves to sustain the reader's interest.

A further literary example of an opening sentence that hooks the reader is found in the Spanish writer Maria Dueñas's novel *El Tiempo entre Costuras*, published by Atria in New York in 2009. The story opens with *Une máquina de escribir reventó mi destino. Fué una Hispano-olivetti, y de ella me separó durante semanas el cristal de un escaparate*. In Daniel Hahn's translation, *The Seamstress*, the opening sentence reads, "A typewriter shattered my destiny. The culprit was a

Hispano-Olivetti, and for weeks a store window kept it from me" (2012: Penguin Books, London, also published as *The Time in Between*).

An Italian example of an opening that intrigues the reader can be found in Andrea Camilleri's *Il ladro di merendine* (1996, Palermo: Sellerio Editore). In the New York poet Stephen Sarterelli's translation *The Snack Thief* (2005, London: Picador), the story's opening tells us that Montalbano

> woke up in a bad way. The sheets, during the sweaty, restless sleep that had followed his wolfing down three pounds of sardines *a beccafico* the previous evening, had wound themselves tightly round his body, making him feel like a mummy.

By retaining the local name for the fish dish, Sarterelli immediately transports readers into the Sicilian *context* of the story and defines the main character as someone who knows how to enjoy life.

ORGANISATION AND LOGIC

Some authors experiment with the structure of the novel. An example of this is Eleanor Catton's *The Rehearsal* (2008, New Zealand: Victoria University Press), which contemplates the very nature of identity and the boundary between truth and fiction. This is achieved by alternating true events with a play about a high school sex scandal and its repercussions that is staged in a drama school. There are also shifts in the timescale with chapters bearing the headings of days of the week or months of the year but in no apparent chronological order. The characters themselves assume different roles, with the result that readers are not always sure whether they are being themselves or are playing someone else.

One technique that translators of crime fiction need to be aware of is **signposting**. Some writers, particularly thriller writers, use very subtle clues to help readers navigate their way through the plot and understand the route that the writer has taken yet not be able to anticipate the ending. Without such hints, a reader could be dissatisfied by the dénouement. An example of this is embedded in the plot of the film *Planes, Trains and Automobiles*, in which Del Griffith (played by John Candy) tells his bad-tempered and reluctant travelling companion, Neal Page (played by Steve Martin), how much he loves his wife but says he hasn't been home for years and never rings her to say his flight has been cancelled. It is only at the very end of the film that Neal discovers why.

The term *signposting* is also used in academic writing, with students being encouraged to clearly indicate the path that their argument is going to take, by inserting words such as "First," "Second" and "Finally." A useful guide to this can be found in the University of East Anglia's guide *Using "Signpost" Words and Phrases*, available

online at https://portal.uea.ac.uk/documemts/6207125/7632456/Using+signp
ost+words+and+phrases.pdf/4347566d-8b81-49ed-b715-e98d28467fed.

Task 6

Workout with words:

a) Open a book of poetry in your source language and make a note of
   any unusual collocations or even instances of oxymoron that you come
   across.
b) Next time you read a novel in your own source language, look at the
   opening page and make a note of the devices the author uses to hook
   the reader.

If you can find a translation of this novel, try to analyse how effectively
the author's hook is conveyed by the translator.

Pause for thought: How would you deal with an unconventionally struc-
tured source text?
　　Would you stick very closely to the source text structure?
　　How would you justify this decision?
　　If you were translating crime fiction, how would you go about spotting
the signposts that the author has put in to give readers clues to the mystery?
　　Why is it important to choose words from the correct level in the seman-
tic hierarchy when you translate these signposts?

THE RULE OF THREE

When considering the structure of a text, it is useful to reflect on how things seem
to run in threes. No-one is quite sure how this rule works, but it can be found in
many areas of life and helps words to acquire added value. It is even embedded
in the fabric of the present book, which focuses on three aspects of texts: *time*,
context, and *culture*. Both translators and writers find themselves following this
rule instinctively as they practise their craft, but an awareness of how it operates
will enhance the coherence of their work.

　　The **rule of three** is a kind of unwritten magic formula or rule of nature that
works at all levels. An essay, for instance, has *an introduction*, a central section
sometimes referred to as *the main body*, and *a conclusion*. The introduction sets

the scene and explains the context to the ideas that you are presenting, the central section outlines the main arguments for and against your thesis or theory and the conclusion brings all the strands together, exploring the wider implications. An essay without a conclusion fails at this third hurdle. Because it is incomplete, it leaves the reader dissatisfied because of the lack of *coherence*. However good the first two components are, people are left feeling as if they are still waiting to be dismissed from a meeting or lecture.

This rule is found in Eastern as well as Western culture. In Japanese wedding traditions, for instance, the concept of three plays a key role. There is a ritual called "San-San-Kudo" (meaning three, three, nine times) involving three groups: the bride and groom, the bride's parents and the groom's parents. Each person takes three sips of sake from each of three cups in a tier. In Japan, the number three or *san* is considered to be lucky, as is *ku*, the number nine (Source: www. japanesestyle.com/Japanese-Wedding-Traditions-San-San-Kudo-s/907.htm).

A good story usually includes three things: a beginning, a middle and an end. In film scripts and plays, there is most often a three-act structure. A very simple example of this can be found in the story of the *Three Little Pigs*, in which the first pig builds a house of straw, the second builds one from sticks and both are eaten in turn by the wolf, but the third, who builds his house of bricks, is able to survive.

Most heroes or heroines overcome adversity only at the third attempt or are confronted by three problems in succession, each being slightly more serious than the last. In fairy tales, it is a common theme for a character to have three wishes and the turning point often comes with the third wish.

The same thing seems to work not only at a structural level but at conceptual and word-based levels too. To make a point clearer, a writer may repeat it. Repetition of the same word or phrase three times is acceptable, yet saying it twice or four times is generally considered to be poor style.

A writer can exploit the rule of three in different ways by moving up or down the scale of intensity, as in the 1966 Clint Eastwood film *The Good, the Bad and the Ugly*, or by putting together a set of three related things, as in the 1987 film *Planes, Trains and Automobiles*. Alternatively, scriptwriters may combine things that are not normally found side by side. For instance, many film titles make their impact by juxtaposing three unrelated things, such as Steven Soderbergh's 1989 film *Sex, Lies and Videotape* or, to quote a more recent example, the June 2014 release *Pulp, A Film about Life, Death and Supermarkets*. Guy Ritchie's 1998 crime comedy *Lock, Stock & Two Smoking Barrels* is a clever twist on the three-part phrase *lock, stock and barrel* (meaning "completely").

An alternative strategy to repeating something three times, and a subtler way of maintaining cohesion at word level, is to use a lexical (or word-related) technique and find a synonym (a word with a similar meaning, such as *author* and *writer*) or an **antonym** (a word that is opposite in meaning, such as *good* and bad). This serves to maintain a theme that runs through the text and makes it flow. Examples of synonyms in German are *empfinden* and *fühlen* (both verbs mean "to feel") or *senden* and *schicken* (both mean "to send") and *erhalten* and *bekommen* ("to receive/get"). An Italian example is *mandare* and *inviare* ("to send"), though as with many (apparent) synonyms, the specific context or register will indicate which word is more appropriate (in the latter case, *mandare* is more informal than *inviare*).

Another word-based cohesive device that links words together involves choosing words within the same **semantic field** or area of meaning, such as the German *Gerät*, *Vorrichtung* and *Apparat* (meaning "device," "assembly," "apparatus" respectively). Sometimes a writer may select a more general term, such as the German *Blume* (flower) or a more specific term from the same hierarchy, such as *Rose* (rose). This strategy may involve *elegant variation*, a device often used to avoid repeating a name, such as using the qualifying expression *le Florentin* (the native of Florence) in French to refer to Machiavelli. In Italian, *Montecitorio*, for example, is commonly used to indicate the Chamber of Deputies of the Italian Parliament. Another strategy is shifting from a negative to a positive perspective as in a glass that is not *half-empty* but *half-full* (modulation).

Task 7: Can you find more examples that illustrate the rule of three?

Find as many book titles and film titles as you can that feature the rule of three, both in your source and your target language.

Are the three items in your examples related to one another? Do they represent different points on the same spectrum?

DECONSTRUCTING, CONSTRUCTING AND RECONSTRUCTING TEXTS

The earlier chapters of this book concentrated on equipping you with the analytical skills required to **deconstruct** a source text. The practical writing activities you have just been tackling were intended to improve your mastery of "word-craft" and empower you to **construct** texts of your own. The resulting insights into the influence of time, context and culture on how a text evolves should equip you to craft target texts that **reconstruct** a piece of source language writing in a way that does full justice to the author's intentions.

Pause for thought: What have these tasks taught you about your own writing voice?

Which form comes most naturally to you? Poetry? Short stories? Memoirs? Reflective prose? Plays? Which genre would you prefer to write in?

Your personal writing preferences could help you to define the type of texts that you would be best equipped to translate.

Finally, both translators and readers need to bear in mind what Stephen King (2000) refers to in *On Writing* as the "**putative reader.**" In the 2012 paperback edition, pp. 261–265 (London: Hodder), King calls this the "*ideal* reader." Whether you are working on an original piece of writing or translating a foreign author's work, try to imagine someone you admire and respect reading the text you have just completed. Try to re-read it with their critical eyes and highlight any words that seem ill-chosen or out of place. If you can approach all your work in this way, your style will benefit enormously.

The importance of writing skills as one of the core competences needed by translators was emphasised recently in Daniela Ford's article: "Translation Technology: Have Our Core Skills Taken a Back Seat?" This appeared in the Institute of Translation and Interpreting's e-book *Trends in Translation and Interpreting 2019*, where she said,

> Knowing how to use translation technology alone does not guarantee you a job; you still need core translation skills, and this includes being able to write to a professional level in your mother tongue and being able to conduct proper terminology research.

After completing the tasks in this chapter, you should be more able to write to a professional level, but you do not have to stop there. You could carry on writing and at the same time read as widely as you can. You could even join a writers' circle where members regularly read out their work in progress to other writers and receive constructive feedback. The act of reading the texts you have created out loud might seem intimidating at first, but if you have scanned them beforehand with your putative reader in mind, it will be less daunting, and you will gain greater control of your craft. Moreover, the interaction with other wordsmiths will help you to hone your writing style and to identify the approach adopted by an author whose work you plan to translate. There could certainly be an unexpected bonus: your greater rapport with the tools of your craft is likely to lead to a dramatic improvement in the quality of your target texts. If this seems a step too far for now, in the meantime, you could join a reading group, which will give you the impetus to acquaint yourself with as many genres as possible.

Although you need to start work rather than just wait for inspiration, it is important to allow yourself some "*time to stand and stare*," as the early twentieth-century Welsh poet W. H. Davies did in his poem "Leisure" (which can be found at www.englishverse.com/poems/leisure).

This concept is nothing new. One of the most famous figures in European medieval literature was the eleventh-century Austrian poet Walther von der Vogelweide. In his Middle High German poem "Ich saz ûf eime steine" (which can be accessed in the original with a modern German translation at www.minnesang.com/Saenger/walther-texte.html#14_Ich_saz_%FBf_einem_steine), he described how he sat on a rock with one leg over the other, his elbow resting on his knee and his chin and one of his cheeks cupped in his hand. Then he thought very carefully about how you were supposed to live your life in this world. So, before you start to write or translate, it is important to take time, like Walther, to sit and think, or like W. H. Davies to stand and stare and develop a strategy for the project you are about to undertake.

POSSIBLE ANSWERS TO SOME OF THE TASKS

Spotting alliteration, assonance or onomatopoeia

Examples of alliteration in *The Russian Concubine* are *four* and *freight* and *behind* and *bucked*.

Examples of assonance are *white* and *sky*; *steam* and *heaving*.

Examples of onomatopoeia are *growled*, *belched*, *rattled*, *shrieking*.

Task 4: ideas for what you could put in an email or text from Mabbut to a friend

"How about meeting up next Friday? I can't wait to get back down south. No let-up in the winds this past week (gale force seven or eight, I reckon). It's calmer now but my head's still pounding after last night's session. Too much single malt!"

Task 5: lexis-based word-building exercise

Words you could use to describe the touch of soft materials

cushioned, downy, feathery, fleecy, flowing, fluffy, fluid, furry, silky, smooth, spongy, squashy, supple, velvety

And of rough surfaces

coarse, hard, rigid, solid, uneven, unpolished

Sounds heard in an early twentieth-century dockyard

The sigh of steam from a ship's engines,
the clank of chains as a gangway is pulled back on board,
a long toot from a ship's horn,
the chatter of passengers' voices and a child's cries are carried ashore by the wind,
the sound of hammering as crates are nailed down,
the squeal of a winch as the crates are hauled onto a ship.

Conclusion

Our analytical approach in this book has focused on three factors: the *time* of writing and/or of translation; the logistical, linguistic and psychosocial *context*; and the source and target *culture*. We have explored the various ways time, context and culture can influence a writer's view of the world and have considered the choices translators need to make in order to reflect the author's voice as closely as possible. With the aid of a model, we have shown you how to evaluate a source text within the context of the translation brief and prepare a text for translation. The annotated translations and translation comparisons highlight some of the challenges translators face, such as linguistic and cultural change, with the result that a target text appropriate in one century, or decade even, may seem quaint or out of date in the next.

At the same time, as we explained in the Introduction, there are two strands running through the book, reflecting its two perspectives: the analytical and the creative. Despite advances in translation technology and artificial intelligence, translators still need to develop vital thinking skills. The "Pause for thought" sections in this book have been designed to enhance these skills, allowing you to rationalise your translation decisions as you apply the various criteria set out in our model to a range of professional assignments in any field of translation. These tasks can be used by the individual aspiring translator and as a springboard for class discussions.

Yet, thinking skills alone are not enough: good writing is often touched by magic. To recreate this magic, what you need is a creative flair. A few fortunate translators are born able to work wonders with words, but most of us need to foster and hone our writing skills. In Chapter 4, we introduced you to some of the key concepts covered in creative writing workshops and provided exercises that should help you to find your own writer's voice. The best way to learn to write well is through regular practice, preferably in a relaxed social environment. Interacting with other wordsmiths in a writing group and writing for fun removes the pressure to be perfect, which stifles creativity, and there is added value: listening to other authors reading their work and even reading out your own literary efforts will increase your awareness of the sound of words and their effect on the ear.

This could well lead to a startling improvement in your ability to craft an effective target text. Why not join a Writers' Circle and give it a try? If you don't feel confident reading out your own work, you can always translate a passage from one of your favourite authors and share it with other members. Translators, too, have to find a voice that matches the writer and the culture and context of the time in which the story is set. The French-English translator Ros Schwartz explained in a "Dialogue on a Translator's Interventions" (Chapter 1, para. 8) published in *The Translator as Writer* (2007, ed. Bassnett and Bush), "I call the translation process finding a voice." She said that she starts to find a voice after she has revised her first draft and then reads it through as an English text, without reference to the French source text.

Reading work aloud is in itself an excellent tool for checking whether the voice is right and also for achieving translation quality control. It is a technique often used by professional literary translators, such as Nicholas de Lange (a Hebrew-English translator). He told Ros Schwartz that he started out translating the work of Amos Oz by reading his target text aloud to the author, who was then at an early stage in his career. He added, "I still listen very carefully to the sound and if I can, I try to read things aloud" (ibid, Chapter 1, Para 10). Ros agreed that she also reads her translations out loud.

With a number of books by award-winning authors not yet translated, it is still possible for aspiring practitioners of the translator's craft to make a career in literary translation if they have sufficient initiative, dedication and determination. They can, for instance, choose a work from a place or a cultural context that is as yet little known in the canon of world literature, a strategy that proved successful for Deborah Smith, the translator of Han Kong's *The Vegetarian*, which won the Man Booker International Prize in 2016. In Deborah's case, her career path entailed deciding to learn a relatively obscure language, Korean, well enough to be able to translate from it – no mean feat. The 2017 Harvill Secker Young Translator's Prize was awarded to another Korean-English translator, Erica Chung, for her translation of a short story by Han Yujoo.

It is gratifying to see translators gaining greater recognition in the Man Booker International, in which the £50,000 prize money was shared between the author and the translator – in 2017, this was Jessica Cohen, who worked on the English version of Israeli author David Grossman's *A Horse Walks into a Bar*. (The year of writing, 2019, was the last year of sponsorship by the Man Group plc. As of 2020, the award will be known as the International Booker Prize.) Authors themselves are now acknowledging the importance of the translator's role as the channel through which a book written in another language can reach out to a wider audience, including people unable to access it in the source language. In her interview with Rachel Cooke in the *Observer* published on 24 July 2016, Deborah Smith points out that Bae Suah, one of the authors she works with, "doesn't read or speak English but is a translator herself, from German to Korean, and so also has a strong idea of translation as creative writing. She thinks I'm the best judge of how to make a book live in my language."

In 2018, the Man Booker International prize was shared by the Polish writer Olga Tokarczuk and the translator Jennifer Croft, who told the *Guardian*,

> It's not just Polish novels that are enjoying a boost. Sales of fiction in translation were up in the UK by 5.5% last year, with sales of translated literary fiction increasing by 20%. As the UK turns inwards, caught up in an increasingly bitter fight over leaving the EU, readers are looking outwards, with literature from mainland Europe accounting for a large part of the growth.
>
> ("It's a silent conversation": authors and translators on their unique relationship," www.theguardian.com/books/2019/apr/06/its-a-silent-conversation-authors-and-translators-on-their-unique-relationship, accessed on 20.05.19)

In 2019, the final year of the Man Group's eighteen-year sponsorship of the Man Booker International prize, the award went to the first female Omani novelist to be translated into English, Jokha Alharthi, for *Celestial Bodies*, translated by Professor Marilyn Booth (Sherwin, A., writing in The *i*, 22 May 2019: 21).

Some forward planning might be required to determine which country's language and popular literature is likely to be of interest in five years' time. Alternatively, the translator can choose a time of historical significance. Just as a journalist will identify a significant anniversary that will appear on next year's calendar and start researching an article on it, the translator may seek to determine whether there are any key works relating to a period of historical significance not yet available in the target language. For example, Alison Flood announced in the *Guardian* on 22 August 2017 that Marian Schwarz's translation of the first of six volumes of *The Red Wheel*, Solzhenitsyn's Russian Revolution epic, was to be published in English in November 2017, celebrating the centenary of the revolution.

On a similar note, a book by a disabled gay writer, which was banned by the Nazis in the 1930s, Friedo Lampe's 1933 novel *Am Rande der Nacht (At the Edge of Night)* has finally been published by Hesperus Press in an English translation by Simon Beattie, as reported in the March-April 2019 edition of the ITI Bulletin.

Not only are translators acquiring a higher profile, but lesser-known cultures and languages are also attracting attention, some for the first time ever. Claire Armitstead, writing in the *Guardian* about fiction in translation on 6 April 2019, after interviewing various authors and translators, asked,

> What of those languages that are the product of cultures with little common ground? The traditional answer has been that they rarely get translated, though research commissioned by the Man Booker International prize revealed the situation to be slowly improving, with a growing demand for Chinese, Arabic, Icelandic and Polish.

She pointed out that the first Uzbek novel ever to be translated into English, Hamid Ismailov's *The Devils' Dance*, was awarded the EBRD (European Bank for Reconstruction and Development) prize in 2019. The translator, Donald Rayfield, was linked up with the author by a new translator-run publishing house, Tilted Axis, set up by Deborah Smith to champion neglected languages.

Commercially sponsored high-profile international prizes have helped to promote world literature in translation. Publishers and professional associations, academics and individuals can all play a part in ensuring that the reading public continues to embrace work from around the world. For the literary blogger and author Ann Morgan (2015: 245), who decided to mark the London Olympics in 2012 by spending the year reading her way around the world (by choosing a book to read from each nation), the relationship between the reader and the translator is based on trust:

Depending on a third person to bring us something from a place we are unable to venture on our own is an act of faith.

Alongside work from little-known writers and cultures, translations of classics from ancient times still enjoy considerable popularity, with the British-born classicist Emily Wilson becoming, in November 2017, the first woman to translate Homer's *Odyssey* into English. Her use of contemporary language and her awareness of the need to spark the reader's interest in Odysseus become evident from the very first sentence: "Tell me about a complicated man." In an interview with Wyatt Mason for the *New York Times Magazine*, on 2 November 2017, she explained her relationship to the Greek source text as follows: "I want to be saying, after multiple different revisions: 'This is the best I can get toward the truth.'" Surely, this is what all translators are striving for. Some insight into the writing process can only bring them closer to this goal.

Appendix

In this section, we have included, where appropriate, some reference material relating to texts quoted in the book. It includes source language originals for some of the texts quoted in translation and commentaries supplied by one of the translators we have featured together with specimen answers to an editing task. We have also added some material that we consider to be of potential benefit to readers, such as original texts and translations produced by experienced professional translators.

REFERENCE MATERIAL

German original for Mies van der Rohe film extract: see p. 50.

In meinem langen Leben habe ich immer danach gesucht worum es sich eigentlich dreht bei der Baukunst.

Und ich bin mehr und mehr zu der Überzeugung gekommen, dass die Baukunst unsere Zivilisation ausdrücken soll, in ihren wesentlichen Teilen.

Nicht in den nebensächlichen Wünschen, sondern das Essenzielle sollte herausgearbeitet werden.

Und das sehe ich als die eigentliche Aufgabe der Baukunst an.

Es ist zwar ein langer Prozess und alles was ich gemacht habe, hat sich darum gedreht, das zu klären. Schritt für Schritt.

So, man kann nicht am Montag morgen eine neue Baukunst erfinden. Das ist etwas naiv.

Baukunst war immer eine ganz ernste Sache. Man hat die Epochen danach benannt.

Und so wird es bleiben!

Italian original for (translation) editing task II: see p. 102.

Storia del Palazzo

Palazzo Gianfigliazzi, affacciato su Lungarno Corsini, costituisce il nucleo piu importante delle numerose case appartenute all'omonima famiglia fino alla fine del Settecento.

Sull'elegante edificio coronato da un'ampia loggia, dal 1427 nel corso dei secoli furono eseguite numerose ristrutturazioni.

Nel 1818 con l'estinzione dei Gianfigliazzi, il Palazzo venne destinato ad albergo, con la denominazione "Delle Quattro Nazioni".

Qui furono ospiti personaggi illustri tra i quali Alessandro Manzoni che, riferendosi all'Arno scrisse la famosa frase "nelle cui acque risciacquai i miei cenci".

Vi soggiornò per lunghi periodi Luigi Bonaparte Re di Olanda il quale diventò proprietario dell'immobile nel 1828.

[. . .] Qui nacque e venne ospitata per molti anni Virginia, giovane Contessa di Castiglione, nota per il suo fascino nonchè per la sua amicizia con Napoleone III di Francia.

Noto sia per gli arredi che per i fastosi ricevimenti, Palazzo Gianfigliazzi diventò uno dei salotti piu brillanti ed esclusivi della città, al punto che venne citato da Hippolite Taine nel suo *Voyage en Italie*, perchè formava *la parure di Firenze*.

Extract from Storia del Palazzo (accessed 2018).
www.hotelbretagna.net/?act=storia&l=it

Italian original for *Tornare nelle Murge* by Carlo Castellaneta: see p. 42.

La strada adesso scendeva: quasi a capofitto dopo un'ultima curva dentro la conca degli ulivi, e la vallata si apriva davanti al parabrezza come se fosse servita sui palmi di due mani.

Due mani aperte, pensò l'uomo al volante. Diede un primo colpo di freno, e poi un altro, prima di fermarsi del tutto sul ciglio della strada. Aveva perso il conto di quante centinaia di chilometri avesse percorso dal giorno in cui si era messo in viaggio. Il paese era ancora lontano, ma quei colori, o forse semplicemente il biancore abbagliante del mezzogiorno, lo avevano costretto ad arrestarsi, come accade a chi, prima di giungere a un appuntamento decisivo, si soffermi per un attimo a raccogliere le idee.

Altre macchine sfrecciavano a tratti, ma nel silenzio tra un passaggio e l'altro c'era nell'aria una specie di fremito, una vibrazione enorme che sembrava far tremare l'intero paesaggio. Su queste strade non era più tornato da quando, trentacinque anni prima, era venuto in viaggio di nozze, soltanto per mostrare a Silvia com'erano fatto le Murge, e poi via di corsa con la Seicento fino a Brindisi, per non perdere il traghetto per Patrasso.

Si può provare nostalgia per una terra che ti ha costretto a partire? Suo padre aveva trasferito la famiglia al Nord quando lui era ancora ragazzo, e c'erano mosche dietro le tendine, tante mosche che non volavano quasi più, intontite anche loro dal caldo, e si lasciavano schiacciare con le dita sul vetro.

Russian original for first extract in Chapter 3, Part 4 Editing Translations from *The Anglo-Saxon Zugzwang: The Irrational Paradox of the Enlightenment* (Golik, N. and Izvekov, A. 2018: 12)

Культура общества есть показатель его "качества" и способности установления "порядка из хаоса". Динамика трансформации культуры может быть различной: развитие, совершенствование, стагнация, кризис… Последнее стало принято понимать как переходное состояние от одного качественного состояния культуры к другому. Теоретическая постановка темы кризисного развития культуры впервые была осуществлена на рубеже XIX – XX веков. Именно тогда слово "кризис" появилось во все более увеличивающемся со временем спектре исследований. Наряду с ним использовались другие определения, звучавшие еще более угрожающе: "закат", "смерть", "катастрофа". В то время много было тех, кто посчитал, что человек вовсе не стал счастливее от успехов антипода культуры – цивилизации. Подобные мысли нашли свое отражение в философских, социологических, исторических работах, литературе и искусстве, в воспоминаниях ученых, политических и общественных деятелей. Этот пласт саморефлексии европейской культуры поистине огромен и во всей своей совокупности бескомпромиссно свидетельствует о наличии признаков осознания кризиса.

По мнению Карла Манхейма, механизм трансформации современной культуры связан с вытеснением "свободных форм" формами диктатуры, если "демократическое массовое общество предоставлено самому себе". В неэкономической, культурной сфере происходят те же процессы, которые характерны для монополизирующегося рынка, и ей также угрожает опасность. Аналогия не случайна. Культура, как и экономика, есть сфера производства – производства культурных ценностей. Разница состоит лишь в том, "что в области культуры эти процессы измеряются иными масштабами."

Russian original for extract used for translation-editing task (2018: 104–5)

Не обращая внимания на близорукость сильных мира сего, и переворот, и его последствия стали превращаться в универсальное явление: возникновение нового типа личности происходит и в других культурах. Теперь не только на Западе, но и на Востоке очевидны признаки появления нового человека – духовно свободного и должного отвечать за свободу, что наглядно демонстрируют реалии XXI в. Причем "демократия" если и имеет к этому отношение, то действительно только вторичное. Экзистенциальная свобода и политические свободы далеко не одно и то же. Свободно образованный личностный смысл и формальные правила, способствующих взаимодействию, находятся в разных и непересекающихся плоскостях. Кроме того, политически несвободный способен быть при этом свободным духовно и наоборот. Поэтому последствия экзистенциального переворота могут быть лишь дополнены формированием современного понимания демократических принципов.

SPECIMEN ANSWERS TO EDITING TASK

Revised version of text translated from Russian (the edits are underlined so that you can compare this text with the version in Chapter 3)

Despite the shortsightedness of the <u>powerful</u> in this world, both the revolution and its consequences are becoming universal: a new type of individual is also emerging in numerous cultures. Both in the West and in the East, there are obvious signs of a new individual <u>emerging</u> – intellectually free and responsible for his freedom, which the realities of the twenty-first century clearly demonstrate. Democracy, if mentioned at all, is of secondary relevance. The existential <u>form of</u> freedom and the political <u>form</u> are far from being the same. A freely-emerged <u>meaning of personality</u> and interaction-favoring formal rules do not overlap. Besides, one can be intellectually free <u>while</u> being politically dependent – and vice versa. Therefore, the consequences of the existential revolution may only be supplemented by the modern-day interpretation of democratic principles.

Heavily edited version of the same text (showing the kind of changes that the editor of a political textbook might make before publication in the UK)

Despite the shortsightedness of those who wield power in this world, both the existential revolution and its consequences are becoming universally evident: at the same time, a new type of individual is emerging in numerous cultures. Both in the West and in the East, there are obvious signs of the emergence of this new individual – one who is intellectually free and responsible for his freedom, as is clearly demonstrated by the realities of the 21st century. Democracy, if the concept is mentioned at all, is of secondary importance. The existential and the political forms of freedom are far from being identical. There is no overlap between a freely emerged meaning of personality and interaction-favouring formal rules. Moreover, a person can be intellectually free yet be politically dependent – and vice versa. This means that the consequences of the existential revolution can only be enhanced by a modern take on democratic principles.

Can you find the changes the editor made and analyse the possible linguistic and stylistic reasons for making them?

ADDITIONAL MATERIAL

Social science text

This extract is taken from "Le protestantisme est-il à l'origine des libertés modernes?" by Valentine Zuber (published in R500, 30 June 2017). The English translation by Ann Pattison "Is Protestantism the source of modern freedoms?" appeared in the *Journal of the Interdisciplinary History of Ideas* Vol 7 no 13 (2018).

La filiation directement religieuse de la Déclaration des droits de l'homme et du citoyen, via la Révolution américaine inspirée par les écrits de John Locke ou les théories para-protestantes d'un Genevois comme Jean-Jacques Rousseau, ne semble pourtant plus faire aucun doute. Ce n'est qu'au lendemain de la seconde guerre mondiale, que le mythe de l'apport privilégié du protestantisme à la définition des libertés moderne a été remis sérieusement en question par les auteurs et penseurs protestants. L'histoire douloureuse de la faillite d'un certain protestantisme face aux menées liberticides et criminelles du totalitarisme nazi y a été pour beaucoup. Les théologiens réformés plaident alors pour une attitude plus humble, en relativisant le mythe protestanto-libéral élaboré tout au long du XIXe siècle. Mais ils s'attachent toujours à la promotion et à la réappropriation par le protestantisme des idéaux humanistes qu'il a contribué à introduire dans l'histoire de la pensée théologico-politique occidentale. Cette adhésion aux libertés modernes incarnées par les droits de l'homme contemporains, ne doit pas faire oublier, selon eux, leur ancrage premier dans le respect du droit de Dieu, seul garant des droits de tous les hommes.

There no longer seems to be any doubt, however, regarding the direct religious lineage of the Declaration of the Rights of Man and of the Citizen, via the American Revolution, which was inspired by the writings of John Locke or the para-Protestant theories of a native of Geneva like Jean-Jacques Rousseau. It was only in the aftermath of the Second World War that the myth of Protestantism's contribution to the modern definition of freedoms was seriously challenged by Protestant writers and thinkers. The painful history of the failure of a certain version of Protestantism to face up to the freedom-curbing and criminal actions of the totalitarian Nazi regime played a considerable part in this. Reformed Protestant theologians then pleaded for a more understated attitude, putting into perspective the Protestant-liberal myth that had been perfected all through the 19th century. Yet they still remained devoted to the promotion and re-appropriation by Protestantism of the humanistic ideals that it helped to introduce into the history of Western theological/political thought. This adherence to the modern freedoms enshrined in present-day human rights must not allow us to forget, according to these theologians, that human rights are primarily anchored in the respect of God's law, which is the sole guarantor of the rights of all men.

***

Ian Higgins has kindly allowed us to use the following extremely helpful notes explaining his translation choices in Apollinaire's poem *The Horseman's Farewell*: see p. 35.

The Horseman's Farewell

Even taken out of context, the poem is striking in its tight formal perfection: it's all in octosyllables, with an orthodox rhyme scheme. This formal perfection is even more striking, almost astonishing, if you take the poem in the context of the collection in which it was published, *Calligrammes*, in which many of the poems are laid out in the shape of things they are talking about, and most of the others are in free verse.

This tight formal structure has two main effects:

(1) It's analogous to the closed-in perfection of the girl's world;
(2) It contrasts with the explosiveness of the content:

- the pun in "Ah Dieu" ("I'm so happy") vs "Adieu" (not even "Au revoir" – just "goodbye"): things aren't at all what they seem;
- the brutal jumps in tense, from present to *passé simple*, and then that tragic imperfect: he's dead, and she's still chuckling in happy surprise.
- the jump to the imperfect coincides with the only enjambment in the poem, a sudden break in the orderly matching of syntax to prosody.

In the Great War context, the poem's like a grenade or a shell – closed in, ready to explode. Therefore, in translating it, I wanted a similarly explosive content. But also, because of its expressive function in the ST, I wanted to give prosody as high a priority as content, a tight formal perfection *to* get a similar effect – an orthodox metre, and if possible a regular rhyme scheme.

But insisting on rhyme can lead you dreadfully astray, and the shorter the line, the more obvious the rhyme and the greater the risk of the tail wagging the dog.

The big dangers are of it looking like a heavy-handed parody or turning into unintentionally comic doggerel.

I found I couldn't get a full rhyme scheme without the comic doggerel effect. But I did manage to get a kind of formal framing, starting with "thing/ring" and finishing with "gate/fate."

The assonance in "lazy days" does service for the alliteration in "longs loisirs," and the near-miss of "days" and "breeze" does something to preserve the ST connection between his "loisirs" and her "soupirs" (assuming the "vos" is addressed to her, which is certainly not explicit).

Even so, the tail does wag the dog to some extent: "gate" certainly gives a rhyme with "fate" (fate's absolutely vital – ideally of course it would be "destiny," but there's no useful rhyme for "destiny," so "fate" is next best), but there is no gate in the ST; however, "gate" does at least fit narratively: he goes through the gate and then turns off, out of sight.

Why "smiling" though? "Laughing" would of course fit just as well metrically, but "laughing at" suggests a jollity and a touch of mockery that the ST "riait au" doesn't imply: in the ST, she's laughing out loud in delight at what's just happened; he's been on leave, perhaps – has he slipped the ring on her finger and proposed to her? Whatever the precise scenario, "smiling" conveys the ironic contrast between the sunny mood she's in as, unbeknown to her, he's killed at the front.

Similarly, mounting, arriving and sitting at home aren't in the ST: they're there for three reasons:

(1) They do at least give an assonance ("go/home"), for want of a satisfactory rhyme; and they give metrical regularity. Also, "mounted" compensates for the loss of "boute-selle" (the trumpet signal to mount), for which, again, I couldn't find an acceptable rhyme.

(2) They help to convey the impact of "mourut là-bas" – là-bas is a really hard word to translate, especially once I've got him going out through the gate: he died "over there"? "out there"? – where – just round the corner? In next door's field? For British people, certainly in 1915, "over/out there" might easily imply across the Channel or in India. Hence, he "arrived" (at his destination, "là-bas") and "died" (there).

(3) Ending the penultimate line with "she at home" corresponds to the only ST line that isn't end-stopped; "tandis qu'elle" is the only enjambment in the otherwise flawless prosodic orderliness: coming after the contrastive "tandis que," the break after "elle" introduces a real fracture and real suspense – what's she doing? This gives the matter-of-fact last line, with its tragically ironic imperfect tense, even more emotional impact. In the TT, breaking the clause after "while she at home" introduces an analogous fracture, suspense and impact.

Overall, then, there's certainly a marked loss, if only because of the added local colour. But I hope it's not gratuitous, because it does fit the context, and I did want to do as the ST does, giving prosody as high an expressive priority as content.

***

We have included here a short but very dense poem by Francis Ponge together with a translation by Ian Higgins and a selection of translator's comments that give considerable insight into how he arrived at the final English version (Francis Ponge: *Le Parti pris des choses* suivi de *Poêmes*, Paris, Gallimard, "Poésie", 1967: 37).

Les Mûres

Aux buissons typographiques constitués par le poème sur une route qui ne mène hors des choses ni à l'esprit, certains fruits sont formés d'une agglomération de sphères qu'une goutte d'encre remplit.

***

Noirs, roses et kakis sur la grappe, ils offrent plutôt le spectacle d'une famille rogue à ses âges divers, qu'une tentation très vive à la cueillette.

Vue la disproportion des pépins à la pulpe les oiseaux les apprécient peu, si peu de chose au fond leur reste quand du bec à l'anus ils en sont traversés.

***

Mais le poète au cours de sa promenade professionnelle, en prend de la graine à raison: "Ainsi donc, se dit-il, réussissent en grand nombre les efforts patients d'une fleur très fragile quoique par un rébarbatif enchevêtrement de ronces défendue. Sans beaucoup d'autres qualités – *mûres*, parfaitement elles sont mûres – comme aussi ce poème est fait."

Blackberries[1] (translated by Ian Higgins)

On the typographical bushes that[2] the poem constitutes along[3] a road leading neither[4] away from *things* nor to the *mind*, a certain fruit[5] is formed from an agglomeration of spheres a drop of ink quite fills.[6]

***

A clutch of black, pink and khaki, they offer more the sight[7] of the various ages of a family of sticklers[8] in all its polished rudeness[9] than any very keen[10] temptation to pick.[11]

In view of[12] the disproportion of pips to pulp, birds appreciate them but little, for little in the end is left them when they have from beak to anus been gone right through.

***

But the poet, on his professional ramble,[13] rightly picks an example and lets it bear seed[14] in his mind: 'So it is,' he says to himself, 'that the patient efforts of a flower which, while defended[15] by a rebarbative tangle of brambles, is very fragile, in great numbers succeed. Without many other qualities, – black blackberries are ripe, exactly, ripe blackberries are black – just as this poem is now exactly right.'[16]

Selected points of interest from Ian Higgins's commentary in French on how he tackled this extremely challenging poem have been paraphrased in the following notes.

NOTES

1 In the French text, it is not clear until line 4 at the earliest whether the poet is referring to *blackberries* or *mulberries*. The English translator, however, is forced to specify the fruit in question from the very start.

2 To avoid the potential confusion that English parataxis might cause in the TT, *that* has been inserted.

3 *Along* was chosen because it is more dynamic than *on* and, combined with the present participle *leading*, prolongs the tension of the paradox of movement and stasis.

4 *Neither . . . nor* is stronger than the French *ne . . . ni* so as to preserve the ST emphasis on *things* and *mind*.

5 The singular form *fruit* was required in English because the plural form *fruits* would refer to a number of different fruits rather than a plurality of one fruit.

6 It was essential to place the stress on *fills*, as the poet does by ending his sentence with *remplit*, hence its final position in the sentence.

7 *Sight* was chosen rather than *spectacle* to avoid a potentially distracting excess of hard "k" and "kl" sounds (as in *clutch*, *black*, *khaki*, and later on, *sticklers*).

8 The key ideas conveyed by the polysemic word *rogue* are *stiffness* and a *cluster of eggs* (as in the roe of a fish) and the fact that there is a play on words because the word has these two meanings. The choice of *sticklers* has the advantage of conveying the connotations of *stick* and *prickles* in addition to echoing the "kl" sound again.

9 The unusual collocation *polished rudeness* is another choice that reflects the duality inherent in Ponge's poem and in the nature of the fruit itself. *Polished* implies calculated perfection and "rudeness" has the root meaning of "roughness" here. It also helps to compensate for losing the **polysemy** of *rogue*.

10 The adjective *vive* is a further example of the duality in the source text, since the temptation is an external impulse, whereas *vive* would normally be used to describe an internal impulse because it usually qualifies a desire or a need. *Keen* captures the essence of this little paradox.

11 The monosyllabic infinitive form *pick* was chosen here instead of the gerund *picking* because *picking* would extend the duration of *la cueillette*, whereas *pick* is analogous to the sound of the abrupt ending of the line in the French text.

12 Since the poet uses the feminine form *vue*, it would be incorrect to translate this as *given* (= *vu*). To translate it as *seeing* would also be misleading, as it would appear to refer to what the birds are doing; *in view of* covers the meaning of the preposition *vu* but also has the overtones of what is seen (the noun *view*).

13 The choice of *ramble*, with its strong connotation of *bramble* in this context, is part of the translator's strategy to compensate for the loss of the effect of the French homonym *mûres*, with its dual meanings of *blackberries/mulberries* and *ripe*.

14 There is a further play on words with *en prend de la graine*. In the French text, this can be read as the idiom meaning to follow someone's example, or it could be taken literally. The translator has covered both bases with *picks an example and lets it bear seed in his mind*. The addition of *in his mind* renders explicit in English what was only implicit in the French text, because the image would not be clear without this.

15 *Defended* needs to qualify *flower* rather than *efforts*, which is why this sentence had to be restructured, with *succeed* being moved to the end.

16 The ending *exactly right* was chosen by way of compensation, the repetition of *exactly* echoing the French repetition intrinsic in *parfaitement* and *fait* and fulfilling the function of stressing at the end of the text, as in the ST, that the blackberries have been perfected in a perfectly finished poem.

Glossary

Some of the following definitions are directly cited from Thinking Italian Translation Second Edition *(Cragie, Higgins et al., Routledge, 2016: 189–196). These are indicated by an asterisk (*) immediately after the glossary term. Other definitions are cited from* Thinking English Translation *(Cragie & Pattison, Routledge 2018: 118–124). These are indicated by a double asterisk (**) immediately after the glossary term. Quotations from other authors are referenced in the respective glossary entries, with full details set out in the Bibliography.*

alliteration** the repetition of a sound, usually of a consonant or consonant cluster, often of an initial consonant, within words that appear in close proximity to one another.

ambiguity** a situation in which either the **ST** or the **TT** can be interpreted in two different ways.

anachronism an item or reference belonging to an earlier period, considered to be outdated or old-fashioned in the new context of writing or speaking.

anaphora** a back reference to an item or items already mentioned.

antonym** a word that is opposite in meaning.

archaic/archaizing (language) lexis or style evoking earlier or historical language or created to produce a period effect.

assonance** the repetition of a sound, usually of a vowel sound, within words that appear in close proximity to one another, often intended to achieve a melodious effect.

backstory significant events and experiences in the characters' past lives that occurred prior to the time in which the narrative is set but which may often explain the motives for their behaviour.

clarity** the ability to express a message in simple and unambiguous terms.

cliché a word or phrase that is so overused in everyday language it has become meaningless, such as "blue sky thinking."

cognitive deficit lack of understanding caused by insufficient contextual information.

cognitive inputs** items of information stored in the individual's memory which make up the cognitive environment.

coherence** the underlying structural links between the ideas within a text. In combination with cohesion, it determines the cogency of an argument.

cohesion** the surface-based structural links between the words within a text that make it flow smoothly by means of lexical or grammatical devices.

collocations** the use of words (a noun and an adjective, a noun and a verb, a verb and an adverb) in combination. Where a non-standard collocation is used, this will attract the reader's attention.

communicative translation* a mode of free translation whereby **ST** expressions are replaced with their contextually/situationally appropriate cultural equivalents in the **TL**; i.e., the **TT** uses situationally apt target-culture equivalents in preference to **literal translation**.

connotation** an overtone, implication or associated meaning embodied by a word.

context** (adj. **contextual**) the cultural background to a text and/or the professional framework to the translation task.

contextualisation** provision of a meaningful context to a text.

creative writing texts produced following a craft-like approach, as opposed to writing for academic, technical, specialist and professional purposes.

critique analysis and evaluation of a literary, philosophical or political theory or work.

cultural share the cultural background or "baggage" of the author or reader that may influence attitudes and approaches to cultural, moral, social and political issues.

culture** the artistic, historical, political and sociological background in the area or areas where a language is spoken.

decoding** understanding the **ST**.

deconstruction reading and analysis of the **ST** aimed at critical awareness, through creation of a platform for identifying characteristics of the **ST** that will be relevant or crucial in the transfer of information, style and cultural aspects from the **SL** into the **TL**.

deep third person a narrative viewpoint that takes readers inside the narrator's head, showing the actions of other characters through the filter of the narrator's reaction to them.

denotation** the primary or literal meaning of a word.

dialect** a regional language variety with non-standard features.

direct transfer (of an SL item into the TL)** preserving the item in its original form, without any modification.

discourse** the ordered and coherent expression of ideas in text or speech.

distant third person a term used by the US author and blogger K. M. Weiland to describe a narrative perspective that sees the action from one character's point of view at a time.

domestication** a term coined by Lawrence Venuti for the process in which the translator brings the TT into line with the target context, making the text seem far less foreign (1995: 20).

duration the relationship between the time it takes for an action in the construct of the narration and the time it takes to narrate the event (a concept developed by Gérard Genette in *Narrative Discourse*, cited in *Literary Theory – the Basics* by Hans Berten, 2014, 3rd ed., Routledge).

dynamic equivalence** a concept developed by Eugene Nida, based on achieving an equivalent or similar effect in the target text whilst sounding as natural as possible (1964: 159, cited in Munday, 2008: 42).

edit** to make a final check before publication of the **TT**, focusing on the style and presentation and ensuring that no typing errors have crept in.

exoticisms** the extensive use of source culture-based terms in the **TT**, matching them to **TL** conventions only where absolutely necessary.

expansion** explanation of the **SL** item in the **TL**.

extra-contextual (references)** the mentioning of items that are extrinsic to the subject matter and immediate context of the **ST**.

faction a formula that enables the author to use a specific historical timeframe and setting, but one in which characters and events are manipulated for dramatic effect.

foreignization** a term coined by Lawrence Venuti for a process in which the translator retains the foreign flavour of the **ST** in the **TT** (1995: 20).

formality** a scale that measures the level of sophistication of the language used in a given social setting.

format (or form)** the physical layout and non-lexical features of a text.

frequency the number of times an event occurs in real life, as opposed to the numbers of times it is narrated (a concept developed by Gérard Genette in *Narrative Discourse*, cited in *Literary Theory – The Basics* by Hans Berten, 2014, 3rd ed., Routledge).

fronting** an action that brings forward information from elsewhere in a sentence.

genre* (or **text-type**) a category to which, in a given culture, a given text is seen to belong and within which it is seen to share a type of communicative purpose with other texts; that is, the text is seen to be more or less typical of the genre.

gloss a brief explanation, usually inserted in brackets into the text, of a word or phrase deemed unlikely to be known or understood by the target readership.

historicism defined in the book of the same name by Paul Hamilton (1996, Routledge) as "insisting on the prime importance of historical context to the interpretation of texts of all kinds."

historic present** the use of the present tense when relating events set in the past.

hook a literary device that is intended to capture the reader's attention from the opening sentence.

hyperonym** a general umbrella term, such as "boat."

hyponym** a specific term, such as "catamaran" or "canoe."

idiolect** an author's own particular style of writing, choice of words, use of figurative language, and tone, sometimes referred to as the author's voice.

idiom** a colloquial phrase with a figurative meaning that goes beyond the literal meaning of the individual words it contains, e.g., to "*bite the dust*," meaning to "come to nothing" or "perish."

inferences** meanings that are suggested or implied "between the lines" in a text, leading the reader to make assumptions.

language structure** the grammatical and syntactic features of a text.

learning outcomes** the skills that students or readers are expected to acquire as a result of attending a course or completing a module.

lexical gap** the absence of a specific term in one language although it may exist in another (in French, for example, the only way of distinguishing between blackberries and mulberries, which are both known as "mûres," is to add the name of the tree the fruit comes from).

lexis (adj. lexical)** vocabulary, terminology or set of words used in a text.

literal meaning** the primary meaning of a word.

literal translation** a word-for-word translation that adheres closely to the **ST** but may sound unnatural and lead to **translationese**.

literary criticism the study, judgement and observations of the quality and interpretation of literature.

literary theory the ideas, principles and methods used to study literature.

localisation** producing a target text in which the cultural content is adapted somewhat to match the target culture.

logline (or **strap-line**) a jargon term used by scriptwriters who want to pitch their ideas to a potential director or film company. To maximise their chance of getting a contract, they try to sum up the plot in a single sentence.

macro strategy** the decisions the translator makes regarding how to approach the particular translation task.

magical realism a literary genre that evolved in South America and in which dreams and magic are interwoven with the fabric of the story.

material culture the physical objects that people can create and attach meaning to (such as clothes and food).

meaning** the set of messages conveyed through discourse, whether spoken or written, both at the level of its individual constituent units and in the text in its entirety.

micro strategies** localised decisions relating to the translation of a word, phrase or other individual unit.

model texts** **TL** texts with similar subject matter or in the same genre as the **ST**, even if the convergence is only partial.

mode of discourse** defined by Mona Baker as "An abstract term for the role that language is playing (speech, essay, lecture, instructions) and for its medium of transmission (spoken, written)" (1992: 16).

monochronic (time) a society that prefers to concentrate on one task at a time, promptness of execution and completion and strict planning.

neologisms newly coined or invented words.

non-material culture abstract ideas not embodied in physical objects: intangible products created or shared by members of a culture over time are aspects of non-material culture (such as social roles, rules, ethics, beliefs, history and behaviour).

omniscient narrator a narrative perspective in which the person telling the story has an unlimited knowledge of everything that is going on.

omniscient third-person point of view see **omniscient narrator.**

onomatopoeia a figure of speech in which a word reflects the sound it describes, such as *roared.*

overmatter superfluous material produced in journalism that can be deleted or saved (i.e., material that might come in useful in the future for a different article).

oxymoron a juxtaposition of words that may appear to be a contradiction in terms, such as the Spanish phrase *silencio atronador* (thunderous silence).

paraphrase** rewording the **SL** item in the **TL** to make the meaning more apparent.

parole a concept developed by Ferdinand de Saussure, who identified individual speech acts as *parole* and the system of differences between signs as *langue.*

pastiche an artistic work that intentionally imitates or evokes the style of another work, for example, a work by an author or an artist.

phrasal verb** a verb combined with a preposition to create a new meaning of its own, such as "bring up" or "check in." Very common in colloquial and informal English.

politeness** a scale that measures where the tone or tenor of the text fits on a scale that ranges from the exceedingly polite to the very familiar.

polychronic (time) a flexible, multi-tasking approach in which relationships are more important than tasks.

polysemy (adj. polysemous)** a situation where a word has a number of possible meanings.

POV (point of view) see **viewpoint.**

processing effort** a term used by cognitive psychologists to describe how hard the brain has to work to assimilate and process information.

purpose (of a text)** to inform, stimulate debate, criticise/praise, recommend, offer an opinion and so on. It may not always be obvious, as in the case of satire, for example.

putative reader a term adopted by Stephen King (2000: 119) to describe a writer's target readership. By visualizing potential readers and examining a draft of a story through the hypothetical eyes of such persons, it is easier to highlight any words that seem ill-chosen or out of place. Translation students have found this technique equally useful when revising their draft translations.

reader-response approach defined by Sonia Colina in *Fundamentals of Translation* (2015, Cambridge University Press) as assessing "the quality of the translation by determining whether readers of the translation respond to it as readers of the source would respond to the original."

reading time any timeframe in which a text is read, whether at the time of publication or subsequently.

reconstruction active engagement and dialogue with the **ST**, leading to transfer into and production of the **TT**.

reduction** simplification and shortening of the **SL** item in the **TL**.

redundancy (i) information expressed more than once and not deemed necessary by the translator in the **TT**; (ii) a lexical item that is considered by the translator or editor to be superfluous in the **TT**.

register** level of language used for a particular purpose or used in a specific setting.

restructuring** an action in which the "shape" of the sentence is changed, in terms of syntax and word-order, to align the **TT** with **TL** discourse conventions.

revision** checking a **TT** (often one produced using CAT tools) against the **ST** for errors, omissions and any inconsistency.

rule of three an unwritten magic formula whereby all good things come in threes.

semantic field** an area of meaning.

semantic translation** an author-centred and more literal translation approach outlined by Peter Newmark (1991: 10–11).

semiology a binary framework developed by Ferdinand de Saussure, who identified individual speech acts as *parole* and the system of differences between signs as *langue*.

semiotics defined by *Oxford Living Dictionaries* as "The study of signs and symbols and their use or interpretation."

sense translation** a technique used to explain the meaning as clearly as possible where a reference, pun or image is not directly translatable.

sentence** "a sequence of words capable of standing alone to make an assertion, ask a question or give a command, usually consisting of a subject and a predicate" (*Collins English Dictionary and Thesaurus 21st Century Edition*).

shape poem poetry that is written or typeset such that it replicates visually the actual shape of the object it describes, a technique popular with the early twentieth-century French poet and artist Guillaume Apollinaire.

signposting the use of subtle clues that hint obliquely at future events and help readers navigate their way through the plot, so they can understand the route that the writer has taken to arrive at the ending.

Skopos theory** a school of thought attributed to Hans Vermeer which, according to Jeremy Munday, "focuses above all on the purpose of the translation, which determines the methods and strategies that are to be employed in order to produce a functionally adequate result" (2008: 79).

SL see **source language**.

social register** the language relating to a specific social setting (level of formality).

sociolect** a social variant of language that is used within a specific social setting.

source language* the language in which the **ST** is expressed.

source text* (or **ST**) the **text** requiring translation.

ST see **source text**.

strategy** the approach adopted by the translator, such as deciding whether to opt for a communicative or semantic translation or a combination of the two.

superordinate** a generic term or **hyperonym**.

suspension of disbelief a state of mind in which a reader is lulled into accepting an improbable or even impossible situation as if it were real, such as a boarding school for trainee wizards.

synonym** a word or phrase with a similar meaning.

syntax** the structure of words into phrases or sentences.

target culture** the cultural, geographical and social setting in which the **TT** will be used.

target language* (or **TL**) the language into which the **ST** is to be translated.

target readership** the readers at whom the target text is aimed.

target text* (or **TT**) the **text** that is a translation of the **ST**.

tenor** an aspect of register that reflects whether the discourse is formal or informal, polite or matter of fact, widely accessible or restricted to a small group of people and personal or impersonal.

text** a coherent piece of writing in a given language.

text-type see **genre**.

theme** existing information about a topic.

TL see **target language**.

translation brief** information relevant to the translation assignment and the intended function of the **TT** that is supplied by the client, work provider or exam setter.

translationese awkward or ungrammatical transfer of words from one language to another, typically as a result of **literal translation**.

translator intrusion** the unwarranted inclusion of the translator's own views in the **TT** and/or the conscious omission of some of the **ST** information content.

TT see **target text**.

viewpoint** the perspective of the text, whether it is fact or allegation, the author's own views and so on.

visualisation** allowing the words to create a picture in your mind.

zeugma** a figure of speech in which a word is used to modify two or more other words in a different sense.

Bibliography

Apollinaire, G. 1915. *"L'adieu du cavalier"* from *Calligrammes*. Paris: Gallimard (1966 edition).

Atkinson, K. 2018. *Transcription*. London: Doubleday.

Atwood, M. 1990. *Cat's Eye*. London: Virago Press.

Baker, M. 1992. *In Other Words*. London and New York: Routledge.

Barry, S. 2014. *The Temporary Gentleman*. London: Faber & Faber.

Bassnett, S. 2007. *The Translator as Writer*. London: Continuum.

Bellos, D. 2013. *Is that a Fish in Your Ear*? London: Penguin Books.

Berten, H. 2014. *Literary Theory: The Basics*. Third Edition. London and New York: Routledge.

Callender, C. 2001. *Introducing Time: A Graphic Guide*. London: Icon Books.

Camilleri, A. 1996. *Il ladro di merendine*. Palermo: Sellerio Editore (Translation in English by Stephen Sarterelli with the title *The Snack Thief*, 2005. London: Picador).

Cannon, J. 2016. *The Trouble with Goats and Sheep*. London: The Borough Press.

Castellaneta, C. 1990. *"Tornare nelle Murge"*. In *Stagioni d'Italia*. Volume 2. Naples: Electa Napoli Srl.

Catton, E. 2008. *The Rehearsal*. Wellington, New Zealand: Victoria University Press.

Choderlos de Laclos, P.A.F. 1985. *Les Liaisons Dangereuses*. London and New York: Routledge (This translation in English by Richard Aldington first published in 1924 by George Routledge & Sons Ltd. with the title *Dangerous Acquaintances*).

Choderlos de Laclos, P.A.F. 1987. *Les Liaisons Dangereuses*. London: Penguin Classics (This translation in English by P.W.K. Stone first published in 1961).

Choderlos de Laclos, P.A.F. 1993. *Les Liaisons Dangéreuses*. Saint-Amand-Montrond: Bussière/Le Grand Livre du Mois.

Choderlos de Laclos, P.A.F. 2008. *Les Liaisons Dangereuses*. Reissued in 2008 (This translation in English by Douglas Parmée first published in 1995 in Oxford's World Classics).

Clark, R. and Ivanič, R. 1997. *The Politics of Writing*. London and New York: Routledge.

Cobley, P. and Jansz, L. 2012. *Introducing Semiotics: A Graphic Guide*. London: Icon Books.

Cocteau, J. 1961. *Les Enfants Terribles*. London: Penguin Books (Translation by Rosamund Lehmann).

Cocteau, J. 1976. *Les Enfants Terribles*. Paris: Le Livre de Poche.

Colina, S. 2015. *Fundamentals of Translation*. Cambridge: Cambridge University Press.

Collins, J. 2011. *Introducing Derrida: A Graphic Guide*. London: Icon Books.

Cragie, S., Higgins, I., Hervey, S. and Gambarotta, P. 2015. *Thinking Italian Translation*. Second Edition. London and New York: Routledge.

Cragie, S. and Pattison, A. 2018. *Thinking English Translation: Analysing and Translating English Source Texts*. London and New York: Routledge.

Culler, J. 2002. *Barthes – A Very Short Introduction*. Oxford: Oxford University Press.

Cullin, M. 2015. *Mr. Holmes*. Edinburgh: Canongate Books.

Dapena-Tretter, A. Autumn 2017. "Jean Dubuffet & Art Brut: The Creation of an Avant-Garde Identity". *Platform*, Vol. 11.

De La Mare, W. *The Return*. 1936. London: Penguin Books.

Dueñas, M. 2009. *El Tiempo entre Costuras*. New York: Atria (The English translation *The Seamstress* by Daniel Hahn, 2012, London: Penguin Books).

Duffy, C. 2011. *The Bees*. London: Picador.

Dumas, A. 1982. *The Three Musketeers*. London: Penguin Classics (Translation in English by Lord Sudley, 1952).

Dumas, A. 1998. *The Three Musketeers*. Oxford: Oxford World's Classics (Translation by William Barrow, 19th century).

Faulks, S. 2018. *Paris Echo*. London: Hutchinson.

Findlay, J. 2015. *Chasing Lost Time: The Life of C.K. Scott Moncrieff: Soldier, Spy and Translator*. London: Vintage Books.

Flanagan, R. 2014. *The Narrow Road to the Deep North*. London: Vintage Books.

Ford, D. 2019. "Translation Technology: Have Our Core Skills Taken a Back Seat?". *Trends in Translation and Interpreting*. Milton Keynes: Institute of Translation and Interpreting (ITI).

Forero, C. 2017. *Entre aquí y allá*. London: El Ojo De la Cultura Hispanoamericana.

Fowler, C. 2017. *The Book of Forgotten Authors*. London: Riverrun.

France, P. (ed.). 2000. *The Oxford Guide to Literature in English Translation*. Oxford: Oxford University Press.

Freely, M. 2006. Translator's *Afterword* to Orhan Pamuk's *The Black Book*. London: Faber & Faber.

Frensham, R. 1996. *Teach Yourself Screenwriting*. London: Hodder & Stoughton.

Furnivall, K. 2007. *The Russian Concubine*. New York: Berkley Books.

Gadamer, G. 1976. *Philosophical Hermeneutics*. Berkeley, CA: University of California Press.

Gansel, M. 2017. *Translation as Transhumance*. New York: Cornell University Press (Translation by R. Schwartz. Les Fugitives Ltd.).

Genette, G. 1980. *Narrative Discourse*. New York: Cornell University Press (English translation).

Glück, I.A. 1998. *Kindheit in Lackenbach*. Konstanz: Hartung-Gorre Verlag.

Golik, N. and Izvekov, A. 2017. *The Anglo-Saxon Zugzwang: The Irrational Paradox of the Enlightenment*. St Petersburg: Altheia.

Hamilton, P. 1996. *Historicism*. London and New York: Routledge.

Harris, J. 2000. *Chocolat*. London: Black Swan.

Hawkins, P. 2015. *The Girl on the Train*. Hull: Riverhead Books.

Heyer, G. 1987. *A Civil Contract*. London: Pan Books.

Hoggart, S. 2012. "Tory Masses Hail Boris as He Swoops into Town". *The Guardian*, 9 October.

Holland, O. and Piero. 2015. *Introducing Literary Criticism: A Graphic Guide*. London: Icon Books.

Honeyman, G. 2017. *Eleanor Oliphant Is Completely Fine*. London: Harper Collins.

House, J. 2016. *Translation as Communication Across Languages and Cultures*. London and New York: Routledge.

Jacobson, H. 2007. *Kalooki Nights*. London: Vintage Books.

Kafka, F. 1917. *Die Verwandlung* (Metamorphosis). Leipzig: Kurt Wolff Verlag. (1933 translation by Edwin and Willa Muir).

King, S. 2000. *On Writing: A Memoir of the Craft*. New York: Pocket Books.

Kushner, T. 2009. *Mother Courage and Her Children*. London: Methuen Drama (A new English translation of Bertolt Brecht's play).

Lathey, G. April 2005. "The Travels of Harry: International Marketing and the Translation of J.K. Rowling's Harry Potter". In *The Lion and the Unicorn*. Volume 29. Baltimore: John Hopkins University Press.

Le Carré, J. 2018. *A Legacy of Spies*. London: Penguin Modern Classics.

Levy, M. 2000. *Et si c'était vrai. . . .* Paris: Robert Laffont.

Manzoni, A. 1972. *The Betrothed*. London: Penguin Classics (Translation by Bruce Penman).

Manzoni. A. 2011. *I Promessi Sposi*. 12th Edition. Milan: BUR.

Marro, E. 2018. "E' Brexodus: ecco dove vanno aziende e banche in fuga dal Regno Unito". *Il Sole 24 Ore*, 6 March.

Marsh, D. 2013. *For Who the Bell Tolls*. London: Guardian Books.

Montesquieu, C. 1721. *Lettres persanes*. Letter 128 (Quoted in Pattison, A. 2006. *Painting with Words*).

Morgan, A. 2015. *Reading the World*. London: Harvill Secker.

Morrison, T. 1987. *Beloved*. New York: Alfred A. Knopf.

Munday, J. 2008. *Introducing Translation Studies*. 2nd ed. London and New York: Routledge.

Newmark, P. 1991. *About Translation*. Clevedon, UK: Multilingual Matters.

Nida, E. 1964. *Toward a Science of Translating*. Leiden: Brill.

Nida, E. 1982. *The Theory and Practice of Translation*. Leiden: Brill.

Orwell, G. 2000. *Nineteen Eighty-Four*. London: Penguin Classics.

Palin, M. 2012. *The Truth*. London: Orion.

Pamuk, O. 2016. *The Naïve and Sentimental Novelist*. London: Faber & Faber.

Pattison, A. 2006. "Painting with Words". In *Translating and Creativity: Perspectives on Creative Writing and Translation Studies*, eds. E. Loffredo and M. Perteghella. London: Continuum.

Pattison, A. 2017. *The Roughs of the Wrythe*. Public performances at Carshalton High School for Girls on 15.07.17, directed by Dick Bower.

Pattison, A. 2018. "New Zealand Rose". Extract published in *Writing on Glass*. London: Caper Press.

Pattison, A. and Sigareva, N. 2009. "The Herzen Human Technology Editing Project". *Modern Concepts of University Education*. St Petersburg: Herzen University.

Pelz, M. 2009. *Memoirs of a German Soldier*. Norderstedt: Books on Demand GmbH.

Pinker, S. 2014. *The Sense of Style*. London: Penguin Books.

Ponge, F. 1967. *Le Parti pris des choses* suivi de *Poèmes* in *Poésie*. Paris: Gallimard.

Poulenc, F. 1989. *Journal de mes melodies* (Diary of My Songs). London: Victor Gollancz Ltd. (French-English parallel text).

Ricoeur, P. 1984. *Temps et Récit*. Volume 2. Paris: Seuil (Translated as *Time and Narrative*, 1985, Chicago: University of Chicago Press).

Robinson, D. 2000. "The Limits of Translation". In *The Oxford Guide to Literature in English Translation*. Oxford: Oxford University Press.

Rotman, P. 2016. *Un homme à histoires*. Paris: Seuil.

Rowling, J.K. 1997. *Harry Potter and the Philosopher's Stone*. London: Bloomsbury.

Rowling, J.K. 1997. *Harry Potter e la Pietra Filosofale*. Florence: Salani Editore (Translation by Marina Astrologo).

Rowling, J.K. 1998. *Harry Potter and the Chamber of Secrets*. London: Bloomsbury.

Rowling, J.K. 1998. *Harry Potter und der Stein des Weisen*. Hamburg: Carlsen Verlag GmbH (Translation by Klaus Fritz).

Rowling, J.K. 1999. *Harry Potter und die Kammer des Schreckens*. Hamburg: Carlsen Verlag GmbH (Translation by Klaus Fritz).

Rowling, J.K. 1999. *Harry Potter y la Cámara Secreta*. Barcelona: Publicaciones y Ediciones Salamandra SA (Translation by Adolfo Muñoz García and Martín Azofra).

Sardar, Z. 2010. *Introducing Cultural Studies: A Graphic Guide*. London: Icon Books.

Sherwin, A. 2019. "Omani Author Wins Man Booker International". The *i*, 21 May, print edition.

Short, P. 2013. *Mitterrand*. London: Bodley Head.

Spufford, F. 2017. *Golden Hill*. New York: Rowohlt (German translation by Jan Schönherr).

Strunk, W. Jr. 1918. *The Elements of Style*. New York: Harcourt.

Süsskind, P. 1985. *Das Parfum*. Zurich: Diogenes Verlag.

Thomas, D. 1953. *The Collected Poems of Dylan Thomas, 1934–1952* (revised edition 1956). London: J.M. Dent & Sons.

Tomalin, C. 2017. *A Life of My Own*. London: Viking Books.

Truss, L. 2003. *Eats, Shoots and Leaves*. London: Profile Books.

Venuti, L. 1995. *The Translator's Invisibility: A History of Translation*. London and New York: Routledge.

Waal de, E. 2010. *The Hare with Amber Eyes*. London: Chatto & Windus.

Widal, A. 1860. *Scenes of Jewish Life in Alsace: Village Tales From 19th-Century France* (which appeared on US translator Steve Capsuto's online blog).

Wilde, O. 1957. *Salomé*. London: Folio Society (Translation by Vyvyan Holland).

Wright, C. 2016. *Literary Translation*. London and New York: Routledge.

Young, S. 2009. "Making the 'Unstageable' Stageable: English Rewritings of Chekhov's First Play". *Modern Drama*, Vol. 52, Issue 3, ISSN 0026-7694, 1 October.

MATERIALS ACCESSED ONLINE

Please note: dates in brackets relate to year of access to the site.

"Après trente ans d'absence, retour triomphale de Georges Mathieu à New York". De Rochebouët, B. www.lefigaro.fr/culture/encheres/2019/01/10/03016-20190110ARTFIG00267-apres-trente-ans-d-absence-retour-triomphal-de-georges-mathieu-a-new-york.php (2019).

"Big Up MLE – The Origins of London's 21st Century Slang". Varghese, S. www.hurriyetdailynews.com/german-teens-pick-up-on-turkish-slang-14827 (2018).

Brainy Quote: www.brainyquote.com/authors/claude_debussy (2019).

"The Burning Chambers". Mosse, K. www.womensprizeforfiction.co.uk/reading-room/find-your-next-read/qa-kate-mosse-new-novel (2019).

Collins Reverso Dictionary: www.reverso.net/text_translation.aspx?lang=EN.

"Damascus and Cairo: Two Heads of Hussein for Two Kinds of Worship". Luizard, J. www.asafas.kyoto-u.ac.jp/kias/en/chronicle.html presented on 21 Jan 2018 at *SIAS/KIAS-CNRS Joint Seminar* at Kyoto University.

Die Presse (on *Rivers of London* by B. Aaronovitch, translated into German): https://diepresse.com/home/kultur/literatur/725749/Ben-Aaronovitch_Geisterbahn-durch-London) (2012).

"Eight Shades of Time" in "Viewpoint, Perspective and Time". 1983. Greenway, W. www.writing-world.com, published online by Allen, M. (2017).

Encyclopaedia Britannia: www.britannica.com/topic/deconstruction (2017).

"Everything You Need to Know About Writing a 3rd-Person POV". Weiland, K.M. www.helpingwritersbecomeauthors.com/third-person-pov (2019).

"The First Woman to Translate the 'Odyssey' into English". Mason, W. www.nytimes.com/2017/11/02/magazine/the-first-woman-to-translate-the-odyssey-into-english.html (2017).

The Guardian/The Observer: www.theguardian.com/guardian-observer-style-guide (2018).

"Guide to the Classics: The Icelandic Saga". Wergeland, O. http://theconversation.com/guide-to-the-classics-the-icelandic-saga-63112 (2016).

"Heaney Wins Second Whitbread Prize". http://news.bbc.co.uk/1/hi/uk/618887.stm (2000).

"Ich saz ûf eime steine". Vogelweide, W. www.minnesang.com/Saenger/walther-texte.html#14_Ich_saz_%FBf_einem_steine.

"Introducing Albus Silente: Harry Potter in Translation". Bradley, A. www.theguardian.com/childrens-books-site/2015/sep/11/harry-potter-in-translation-albus-silente-dumbledore (2018).

"Leisure". Davies, W.H. www.englishverse.com/poems/leisure (2019).

Loglines: www.filmdaily.tv/logline/top-box-office-logline-examples (2019).

"Octavio Paz". Thomson, A. http://modernpoetryintranslation.com/poet/octavio-paz (2019).

"Rereading: Doctor Zhivago". Pasternak Slater, A. The Guardian/The Observer: https://www.theguardian.com/books/2010/nov/06/doctor-zhivago-boris-pasternak-translation.

"Scenes of Jewish Life in Alsace: Village Tales From 19th-Century France". Widal, A.; sample chapter of the translation by Capsuto, S. http://betweenwanderings.com/2018/06/free-sample-chapter-scenes-of-jewish-life-in-alsace-village-tales-from-19th-century-france (2018).

"Seamus Heaney's Translation of Aeneid Book VI: A Fitting End to a Life's Work". Balmer, J. www.newstatesman.com/culture/books/2016/04/seamus-heaney-s-translation-aeneid-book-vi-fitting-end-life-s-work (2016).

The Telegraph: www.telegraph.co.uk/news/2019/05/22/jokha-alharthis-novel-celestial-bodies-wins-man-booker-international.

"Three Sisters". Chekhov. http://muse.jhu.edu.ezproxy.herts.ac.uk/article/361930#b22 (2018).

University of Oxford: www.ox.ac.uk/sites/files/oxford/media_wysiwyg/University%20of%20Oxford%20Style%20Guide.pdf.

"Using 'Signpost' Words and Phrases". University of East Anglia: https://portal.uea.ac.uk/documemts/6207125/7632456/Using+signpost+words+and+phrases.pdf/4347566d-8b81-49ed-b715-e98d28467fed (2019).

"Wild Honey". Chekhov. http://muse.jhu.edu.ezproxy.herts.ac.uk/article/361930#b24 (2018).

ITI BULLETIN ARTICLES

"Beyond Words". Bassnett, S. *ITI Bulletin*, September–October 2018.

"First Translation of Banned 1933 Novel". *ITI Bulletin*, March–April 2019.

"Good Night, Sweet Prince". Bassnett, S. *ITI Bulletin*, November–December 2018.

"Lexicon of a Leader". McCafferty, Y. *ITI Bulletin*, May–June 2017.

"Neither Rhyme Nor Reason". Bassnett, S. *ITI Bulletin*, September–October 2015.

"Visions and Revisions". *ITI Bulletin*, November–December 2018.

Index

Note: Page numbers in **bold** indicate a glossary entry.

Printed in Great Britain
by Amazon

41739316R00097